AF575913

35

NAVAL

USS Indianapolis (CA-35)

From Presidential Cruiser, Delivery of the Atomic Bombs, to Tragic Sinking in WWII

DAVID DOYLE

Library of Congress Control Number: 2020952560

Designed by Justin Watkinson
Type set in Impact/Minion Pro/Univers LT Std

ISBN: 978-0-7643-6262-0
Printed in China

Published by Schiffer Publishing, Ltd.
4880 Lower Valley Road
Atglen, PA 19310
Phone: (610) 593-1777; Fax: (610) 593-2002
E-mail: Info@schifferbooks.com
www.schifferbooks.com

Acknowledgments

This volume will present information that is in some cases counter to other widely published and well-established reports. This is a result of careful and painstaking research into original records held by the US Navy, the National Museum of Naval Aviation, the Naval History and Heritage Command, the Naval History Institute, the late Paul G. Allen, the National Archives and Records Administration, Temple University, and the Independence Seaport Library.

In compiling this history I was truly blessed to have the invaluable help of many colleagues whom I am fortunate to call my friends, including Tom Kailbourn, Scott Taylor, Sean Hert, Tracy White, Rick Davis, and Dana Bell. Their generous and skillful assistance adds immensely to the quality of this volume. I am especially blessed to have the ongoing help of my wonderful wife, Denise, who has scanned thousands of photos and documents for this and numerous other books. Beyond that, she is an ongoing source of support and inspiration.

All photos are from the collections of the US National Archives and Records Administration unless otherwise noted.

Contents

Introduction 004

CHAPTER 1 The Prewar Years 007

CHAPTER 2 Pearl Harbor to Okinawa 051

CHAPTER 3 Kamikaze! 105

CHAPTER 4 *Indianapolis*: Lost . . . and Found 122

Introduction

USS *Pensacola*, lead ship of the Pensacola class, is shown underway at sea in September 1935. Laid down in October 1926, she was the first US cruiser built under the restrictions of the Washington Naval Treaty. Her main battery consisted of ten 8-inch guns divided among four turrets. Built as light cruiser 24, she was redesignated a heavy cruiser in July 1931. *Naval History and Heritage Command*

The Northampton-class cruisers were the immediate predecessors to the Portland-class ships. Designed to meet the Washington Naval Treaty limitations of 10,000 tons, the ships in fact came in underweight. This knowledge influenced the design of the later ships, which featured improvements that took advantage of the additional weight available. This is the lead ship of the class, USS *Northampton*, cruiser 26, shown here in May 1934.

For members of her crew, a warship of any size is much like a community. Hundreds or, in the case of carriers and battleships, thousands of men inhabit these vessels. Unlike pilots, who are in their aircraft for hours and then return to ground, or tankers, who most often camp beside their vehicles, the men of a warship live on the ship for weeks or months on end. They work, eat, sleep, and relax within the confines of their vessel. Unlike residents of a village, they can't leave town—the city limits is a thin wire guardrail separating them from the deep blue sea.

It is likely for this reason that rarely do sailors preface their ships' names with the article "the." Just as when you tell someone where you live, you don't preface the town name with "the"—and neither do the sailors. In fact, the US Navy style guide specifically states that the word "the" is NOT to be used before the ship name. Hence, this book is not about the *Indianapolis* but, rather, is about *Indianapolis*. *Indianapolis* was a community for her crew, where they lived, worked, and laughed, and many would die.

Warship design is always a trade-off, a delicate balance of speed, sea keeping, operational range, armament, and protection, the latter including protection from bombs and high-angle projectiles, low-angle shellfire, and underwater threats of mines and torpedoes. Oftentimes, these factors are at odds with each other; for example, what is good for protection is often bad for speed. The interconnecting factors in all of these are cost and weight.

The August 17, 1923, Washington Naval Treaty imposed strict limits on armament and, more importantly, specified a 10,000-ton weight limit on cruisers. The armament was limited to a maximum of 8-inch guns.

These were the circumstances that brought about the USS *Indianapolis* and her sister ship, USS *Portland*. These ships were born from the Cruiser Act of 1929, ratified February 13 of that year, which initiated a fifteen-cruiser program. The language of the act authorized "Five light cruisers during each of the fiscal years ending June 30, 1929, 1930, and 1931, to cost, including armor and armament, not to exceed $17,000,000 each." Further, the act read, "*Provided*, that if the construction of any vessel herein authorized to be undertaken in the year ending June 30, 1929 or 1930, is not undertaken in that fiscal year, such construction may be undertaken in the next succeeding fiscal year: *And provided further*, that the first and each succeeding alternate cruiser upon which work is undertaken, together with main engines, armor, and armament for such eight cruisers, the construction and manufacture of which is authorized by this Act, shall be constructed or manufactured in the government navy yards, naval gun factories, naval ordnance plants, or arsenals of the United States, except such material or parts as are not customarily manufactured in such Government plants."

The hull numbers of these groups were planned as CA-32-36, CA-37-41, and CA-42 through CA-46, and, as originally planned, this would result in three classes of ships, each class comprising five sister ships.

In accordance with the terms of the Cruiser Act, construction of the ships were assigned to shipyards as follows:

CA-32 New York Navy Yard
CA-33 Bethlehem Shipbuilding Corp., Fore River Shipyard, Massachusetts
CA-34 Puget Sound Navy Yard, Washington
CA-35 New York Shipbuilding Corp, Camden, New Jersey
CA-36 Philadelphia Navy Yard

Design work toward these ships had begun in 1927 and had largely been finalized by 1929.

With that cruiser design complete, the Navy's Bureau of Construction and Repair turned its attention to the next group of cruisers, the CA-37 through CA-41 class. Study of the Navy's previous cruiser designs, which were just being completed, showed that the ships were coming in under the design weight, which meant the new designs could have some improvements that were previously thought to be precluded by weight limitations.

The Navy felt that the new CA-37 design included sufficient improvement to warrant a drastic change in plan, which was introduced on April 25, 1930.

Construction of the two vessels of the CA-32 class to be built in commercial shipyards, CA-33, *Portland*, which had been laid down on February 17, 1930, and CA-35, *Indianapolis*, contracted for on August 15, 1929, and laid down on March 31, 1930, was to proceed as planned. However, the three ships of the class to be built in Navy shipyards would instead be built to the new CA-37 design. This dramatic change would delay completion of those ships by a year and increase cost to $700,000 each.

As a result of this change, CA-33 and CA-35 became a two-ship class, known as the Portland class. Further, the new CA-37 design was so tight that ships of that class could not be fitted as fleet flagships, whereas the CA-33 and CA-35 design had both the space and the weight capacity to be outfitted as fleet flagships, and they were so equipped.

Being relatively new and of impressive size and having flagship capabilities were no doubt all factors that would play into *Indianapolis*'s frequent hosting of dignitaries throughout the 1930s.

Light vs. Heavy Cruiser

The congressional act that authorized the construction of *Indianapolis* specified that she was a light cruiser, and the builder's order, or "Contract for the Construction of *Indianapolis* Light Cruiser No. 35 of not exceeding 10,000 tons standard displacement," so specified. Since almost all literature concerning *Indianapolis* refers to her as a heavy cruiser, it is worthwhile to explain this apparent discrepancy. In July 1920, the United States reclassified its then-existent fleet of armored (designated ACR) and protected (designated C) cruisers as armored cruisers, with the designation CA. In 1921, the former protected cruisers were reclassified again as light cruisers on the basis of their armor protection, which was modest.

Six battle cruisers had been begun in 1920–1921. These six massive ships, to be armed with 16-inch, .50-caliber guns, and displacing 43,500 tons and with a length of 874 feet, were the largest cruisers ever contracted for by the US Navy and were of a size comparable to the nation's largest battleships. While these ships were victims of the 1922 Washington Naval Treaty, with four of the six incomplete hulls being scrapped on the builders' ways, and two, *Lexington* and *Saratoga*, being converted to aircraft carriers, their classification, battle cruiser, remained on the books.

Thus, when the Cruiser Act authorized the construction of fifteen cruisers, they were light cruisers as a result of the US Navy standards at the time, which classified cruisers on the basis of armor.

The 1930 London Naval Treaty changed the standard by which cruisers were to be judged, distinguishing light and heavy cruisers by armament, with anything above 6.1-inch main armament being considered heavy cruisers, while those below that bore were light cruisers. Prior to this instrument, the US Navy had two types of cruisers, battle cruisers and light cruisers.

Various signatories had heavy-cruiser tonnage limits, with the US being allocated eighteen ships totaling 180,000 tons, Britain fifteen vessels with a total of 147,000 tons, and Japan twelve such ships with a total of 108,000 tons. Light cruisers did not have a quantity limit but, rather, tonnage limits, with the US limit for light cruisers being 143,500 tons.

Thus, *Indianapolis* was purchased as a light cruiser, and even though by the time of her launching in November 1931 she was technically a heavy cruiser, the press of the era continued to refer to the ship as a light cruiser for quite some time.

During World War II, the ship and her crew would earn ten battle stars: participation in Pacific raids that included the air action off Bougainville (February 20, 1942) and the Salamaua-Lae raid (March 10, 1942); the occupation of Attu, Aleutian Islands (May 25–June 3, 1943); the Gilbert Islands operation (November 20–December 8, 1943); the Marshall Islands operation, including the occupation of Kwajalein and Majuro Atolls (January 29–February 8, 1944) and the occupation of Eniwetok Atoll (February 17–March 2, 1944); Asiatic-Pacific raids, involving Palau, Yap, Ulithi, and Woleai (March 30–April 1, 1944); the Marianas operation, involving the occupation of Saipan (June 11–August 10, 1944), the Battle of the Philippine Sea (June 19–20, 1944), and the capture and occupation of Guam (July 21–23, 1944); the capture and occupation of Tinian (July 24–25, 1944); the capture and occupation of the Southern Palaus (September 6–October 14, 1944); the capture and occupation of Iwo Jima (February 15–March 6, 1945), Fifth Fleet raids against Honshu and the Nansei Shoto (February 15–16, February 25, and March 1, 1945); and the Fifth Fleet and Third Fleet raids in support of the Okinawa Gunto operation (March 17–25 1945) and the assault and occupation of Okinawa Gunto (March 26–April 5, 1945).

All of this would be overshadowed by the events of July 1945.

The third generation of Treaty cruisers was the Portland class. Although five ships of the class were planned, only two were built, class lead *Portland*, cruiser 33, and *Indianapolis*, cruiser 35. The remainder of the class were instead built to a later design.

CHAPTER 1

The Prewar Years

US Navy cruiser 35, named *Indianapolis*, was constructed by the New York Shipbuilding Corporation, at Camden, New Jersey. Building was formally commenced with the laying-down-of-the-keel ceremony, on March 31, 1930. The ship was launched on November 7, 1931, and she is shown here on the building ways shortly before that event. Part of the superstructure had been constructed.

As previously noted, *Indianapolis* was built by New York Shipbuilding of Camden, New Jersey. Her keel was laid on March 31, 1930, and only twenty months later, on November 7, 1931, she was launched. She was sponsored by Miss Lucy Taggart, daughter of the late Democratic Party chairman, city of Indianapolis mayor, and later senator Thomas Taggart. After another year of fitting out, on November 15, 1932, she was placed in commission at the Philadelphia Navy Yard, with Capt. John Morris Smeallie becoming her first commanding officer.

Indianapolis steamed from Philadelphia on February 13, beginning her 11,000-mile shakedown cruise, stopping at Guantanamo Bay, traversing the Panama Canal, and moving along the west coast of South America before returning to the Philadelphia Navy Yard on April 24. There she was given a post-shakedown overhaul. In May, she underwent standardization and final acceptance trials of Rockland, Maine.

Indianapolis steamed north to the Roosevelt family retreat on Campobello Island, at the Canada-Maine border, and received President Franklin Roosevelt aboard there on July 1, 1933.

With the president aboard, *Indianapolis* steamed for Annapolis, arriving two days later and welcoming six members of the president's cabinet aboard for lunch and a cabinet meeting on July 3. The president went ashore at sunset on Independence Day, and the cruiser returned to the Philadelphia Navy Yard.

From July 29 to August 8, *Indianapolis* lay off Bar Harbor, where members of her crew took part in the International Maritime Tennis Championship, held at the Bar Harbor Club. They competed against HMS *Norfolk* and HMS *Danae*.

The next month, on September 6, 1933, Claude A. Swanson, who in March had been named secretary of the Navy, broke his flag on *Indianapolis*. Steaming for Hawaii with the secretary aboard, *Indianapolis* stopped briefly in Havana, arriving at Colon, Canal Zone, on September 11. After an inspection of the Navy facilities in Hawaii, *Indianapolis*, with Swanson still aboard, steamed to the Puget Sound area, then turned again south, making for San Pedro, arriving on October 24. At San Pedro, Swanson left the *Indianapolis* for an inspection of the frigate USS *Constitution* before retiring his flag from the *Indianapolis* on October 27. Swanson took the train back to Washington, DC.

On November 1, *Indianapolis* became flagship of the Scouting Force, operating in waters off the US West Coast. She would remain the flagship of the Scouting Force until the early days of World War II.

On April 9, 1934, she steamed from Long Beach, taking part in fleet exercises, including the remarkable rushed transit of 110 warships through the Panama Canal in forty-seven hours. In Caribbean waters the ship took part in Exercise N on May 11–12 before steaming for New York City, arriving May 29. Once again, President Roosevelt came aboard and was joined by other dignitaries, and from the *Indianapolis* he reviewed the fleet. *Indianapolis* then joined the other ships of the fleet as part of an 11-mile-long display of US naval firepower in the Hudson River.

Following the naval review, *Indianapolis* with the rest of the fleet steamed for Newport, Rhode Island, before returning to the Caribbean for gunnery exercises, ultimately arriving off Panama on October 22. An east–west rush transit of the canal was made in conjunction with Army exercises, with seventy-nine ships passing through the canal in forty-two hours. After having spent Navy Day in Panama, *Indianapolis* returned to Long Beach on November 9, continuing her role as flagship of the Scouting Force. In December, *Indianapolis* gained a new commanding officer, Capt. William McClintic.

Fleet Problem XVII, which began in April 1935, took *Indianapolis* and her crew from Alaska to Midway Atoll. *Indianapolis* was assigned to the Black Force (nominally representing Japan), operating out of Dutch Harbor, Alaska. The Black Force objective was defending Midway, which presumably had been taken in an earlier operation. At the conclusion of the exercise, *Indianapolis* returned to the West Coast.

In March 1936, Capt. H. K. Hewitt, US Navy, relieved Capt. McClintic, and two months later *Indianapolis* took part in Fleet Problem XVIII, off the west coast of the US, the Panama Canal Zone, and Central America. After that exercise, she steamed to Hampton Roads and Annapolis before entering New York Navy Yard for overhaul on June 10, 1936. She remained in the yard into August, then rejoined the fleet.

She steamed to Charleston, South Carolina, taking aboard President Roosevelt on November 18, 1936. *Indianapolis* hosted the president for his "Good Neighbor" cruise of South America. *Indianapolis* crossed the equator on November 23, with the Pollywogs being initiated by the Shellbacks under the Court of Davy Jones. President Roosevelt, not surprisingly, was not subjected to as extensive of rigors as the other Pollywogs.

Arriving first in Port of Spain, Trinidad, on November 12, then calling on Rio de Janeiro on November 27; Mar del Plata, Buenos Aires, on November 30 for the conference of Pan-American states; and Montevideo, Uruguay, on December 1, *Indianapolis* then returned to Trinidad on December 11. She steamed from Trinidad, returning the president to Charleston on December 15.

Indianapolis steamed for the West Coast in early 1937, and it was there on June 7 that Capt. Hewitt was relieved by Capt. (later admiral) Thomas C. Kinkaid while the ship was undergoing repair at Long Beach.

Indianapolis, along with Cruiser Divisions 4, 5, and 6, sailed for Seattle. She left there on July 15, steaming to Portland, where she remained until July 29, when she steamed toward San Francisco. During this transit she made her annual full-power run, recording 31.7 knots at 348 rpm.

Following ten days in San Francisco, the ship put to sea as part of the Green Fleet for four days of exercises. During this time there was a burial at sea for a sailor killed in a shipboard accident.

From mid-August through mid-October, *Indianapolis* would typically leave Long Beach on Monday, returning on Friday afternoon, with the days at sea being filled with short-range battle practice.

In late October, *Indianapolis* was in Oakland for Navy Day celebrations before entering Mare Island Navy Yard for her three-month-long annual overhaul. While at Mare Island, attack transport *Henderson* (AP-1) hit *Indianapolis*'s stern, damaging a propeller guard and requiring an additional two weeks in drydock 2.

Repairs completed, on March 15, 1938, *Indianapolis* and the Scouting Force steamed as the White Fleet for Fleet Problem XIX in Hawaii. During her return to Long Beach, she refueled four escorting destroyers with 30,000 gallons of fuel each, a new process and an exercise that would serve all well in the future.

Indianapolis was in Elliott Bay on July 4, 1938, with part of her crew participating in a parade in Seattle. She then steamed back to San Francisco, where on July 13, VAdm. Adolphus Andrews relieved VAdm. Tarrant as the commander of the Scouting Force aboard *Indianapolis*, which remained the Scouting Force flagship.

Following a presidential review of the fleet on July 14, conducted by Roosevelt aboard the *Houston* (CA-30), *Indianapolis* plus Cruiser Divisions 4 and 5 steamed north to Portland, where she remained until August 1. *Indianapolis* then steamed back to San Francisco, where RAdm. Husband E. Kimmel came aboard for an official call on VAdm. Andrews. Kinkaid and Kimmel were more than acquainted, since Kimmel was married to Kinkaid's sister Dorothy. *Indianapolis* returned to Long Beach August 12. On August 27, Capt. J. F. Shaforth relieved Kinkaid as *Indianapolis*'s commanding officer.

Shaforth and Andrews maintained much the same routines as their predecessors, with *Indianapolis* again going to Seattle and to Pearl Harbor. When *Indianapolis* put into Mare Island Navy Yard in November 1939 for drydocking and overhaul, it was noted that since commissioning she had steamed a total of 215,140 nautical miles.

In April 1940, *Indianapolis*, along with the rest of the US fleet, was shifted from California to Pearl Harbor, in hopes the move would act as a deterrent to Japanese aggression.

On February 1, 1941, the US Navy was reorganized into three fleets: Pacific Fleet, Atlantic Fleet, and Asiatic Fleet. At that time, VAdm. Wilson Brown, commander of the Scouting Force, also became the commander of Task Force 11, with *Indianapolis* as his flagship. Task Force 11 included USS *Lexington* (CV-2), eight cruisers, nine destroyers, six amphibious assault ships, and several smaller vessels.

Indianapolis is viewed from off her starboard bow not long before her launching. Temporary safety rails have been installed on the edge of the forecastle deck. Cables from the forward poppet are secured to seven pad eyes on the side of the hull. Portholes were present on the side of the hull on the main deck, the second deck, and, just above the waterline, the first platform. Jutting from the superstructure are the floors of the signal bridge (*lower*) and the navigating bridge (*upper*). *Special Collections Research Center, Temple University Libraries, Philadelphia*

The four three-bladed propellers were installed on their shafts before *Indianapolis* was launched. The two starboard ones as well as the single rudder are seen in this photo of the starboard stern shortly before the launching. Forward of the propellers are the aft poppets, supporting the rear of the hull. Jutting from the hull above the outboard propeller is the starboard propeller guard.

Wooden cradles called poppets were secured to the bottom of the bow and the stern to support those parts of the hull during launching. The right front poppet is shown. It was secured in place with numerous cables, attached to the hull. A hydraulic jack to the front of the base of the poppet is available to give the poppet a push upon launching, if necessary.

US Navy ships have sponsors, who christen them when they are launched. For *Indianapolis*, the sponsor was Miss Lucy Taggart, daughter of politician and former Indianapolis mayor Thomas Taggart. She is shown here, *third from left*, with her guests at the launching. *Independence Seaport Museum, Philadelphia*

Lucy Taggart poses for an individual portrait before the christening, with a large bouquet in her left hand and the traditional bottle to break on the bow of the ship, to christen her, in her right hand. *Independence Seaport Museum, Philadelphia*

Indianapolis displays her sleek, modernistic lines in a view of the bow around the time of her launching. The anchors are installed, and American flags are draped on the bow in celebration of the launching. *Special Collections Research Center, Temple University Libraries, Philadelphia*

Indianapolis is making her slide down the two ways at the New York Shipbuilding Corporation shipyard at Camden, New Jersey, on November 7, 1931.

Indianapolis has exited the construction shed and slid free of the ways and into the Delaware River.

The ship is seen from the forward port quarter as it enters the Delaware River. Whereas it was customary in the construction of battleships to mount the turrets and guns during the fitting-out period between launching and commissioning, turrets 1 and 2 and their triple 8-inch/55-caliber guns already have been installed. *Special Collections Research Center, Temple University Libraries, Philadelphia*

Following her launching, the cruiser *Indianapolis* was towed to a New York Shipbuilding fitting-out pier at Camden. There, for the next year, construction and outfitting of the ship would continue. This aerial photo was taken about a month after the launching, on December 5, 1931. The starboard catapult is visible to the outer sides of the smokestacks. *Independence Seaport Museum, Philadelphia*

Indianapolis is viewed from another perspective off her starboard stern on December 5, 1931. Turret number 3 and its guns had been mounted before the ship was launched. By the time this photo was taken, the two smokestacks had been mounted, and scaffolding had been erected around parts of the superstructure. The two forward 8-inch/55-caliber turrets are visible. *Independence Seaport Museum, Philadelphia*

Fitting-out of *Indianapolis* continues at New York Shipbuilding, Camden, New Jersey, on April 1, 1932, five months after her launching. Although the superstructure is encased in scaffolding, the structure has taken shape up to the foretop, which includes the forward fire-control station. The square windows of the pilothouse are visible behind the scaffolding. On the aft smokestack, the searchlight platform is under construction. *Independence Seaport Museum, Philadelphia: Aero Service Collection*

In a July 1, 1932, photograph, a flared bulwark has been installed on the navigating bridge above the pilothouse. This was a distinctive feature of *Indianapolis* and her sister ship USS *Portland* (CA-33) as built. Above that bulwark, on the front of the forward fire-control station, is the forward range clock: a visual device to signal the range to a target to other ships in the line. Behind the flared bulwark on the navigating bridge are two of the three rangefinders installed on that level. The forward rangefinder was used for navigation; the two aft ones were used in conjunction with the fire-control system. *Independence Seaport Museum, Philadelphia: Aero Service Collection*

A month and a half before her commissioning, *Indianapolis* is seen from the aft-port quarter during the painting of the ship at the Philadelphia Navy Yard, on September 18, 1932. The cruiser was being prepared for a precommissioning shakedown cruise to waters off Maine. Above the base of the mainmast, forward of turret 3, is the aft range clock. Above the stern is the flag staff. *Special Collections Research Center, Temple University Libraries, Philadelphia*

Tugboats are assisting *Indianapolis* as she departs from Philadelphia for a shakedown run to Maine on October 18, 1932. *Special Collections Research Center, Temple University Libraries, Philadelphia*

Indianapolis is observed from the starboard side during manufacturer's trials in October 1932. Flying from the mainmast is the corporate flag of the New York Shipbuilding Corporation: "NYS" and one or two illegible letters are visible on it. *Independence Seaport Museum, Philadelphia*

During manufacturer's high-speed trials, *Indianapolis*'s bow is plowing up an impressive wave. The housings for three rangefinders were on the navigating bridge at this time, with the actual rangefinders not yet installed: one at the front and two to the rear. The rear starboard one is in line with the top front of the forward smokestack. An aft rangefinder is on a platform to the immediate rear of the aft smokestack. *Independence Seaport Museum, Philadelphia*

Smoke is pouring out of the aft stack of *Indianapolis* during a high-speed run off the coast of Maine on October 26, 1932. This evidently was the manufacturer's trial, during which the New York Shipbuilding Corporation put the ship through its paces and ensured all systems were in order before delivering the ship to the US Navy. The feature at the top of the foretop, to the front of the foremast, was a Mk. 27 primary-battery director, for controlling the 8-inch/55-caliber guns.

Following trials off the coast of Maine, *Indianapolis* has returned to Philadelphia, where tugboats are maneuvering her to her berth on November 14, 1932. A windshield, tilted out at the top, is on the front and sides of the navigating bridge, one level above the pilothouse. *Special Collections Research Center, Temple University Libraries, Philadelphia*

The commissioning ceremony is underway on the fantail of *Indianapolis* at Philadelphia Navy Yard on November 15, 1932. Members of the ship's initial crew, called the commissioning crew or plank holders, are in attendance. The commissioning was the occasion upon which the ship was formally transferred to the US Navy. While in commission, the title "USS" (United States Ship) appeared before the ship's name. The inset photo shows the first commanding officer of the ship, Capt. John M. Smeallie. *Special Collections Research Center, Temple University Libraries, Philadelphia*

Following her commissioning, the US Navy subjected USS *Indianapolis* to a series of trials off the Atlantic coast, between New York and Hampton Roads, Virginia, to establish data on the ship's performance and to identify any problems with the ship and its machinery. Tugs are coaxing *Indianapolis* out of her berth for the beginning of the trials on a chilly January 10, 1933. *Special Collections Research Center, Temple University Libraries, Philadelphia*

Following postcommissioning sea trials, USS *Indianapolis* departed from the Philadelphia Navy Yard for a shakedown cruise to southern waters. Friends and relatives of crewmen are gathered at the dock to see them off on February 14, 1933. The ship had two catapults amidship on the main deck. Two Vought O2U Corsair scout planes are mounted in tandem on the starboard catapult; another Corsair is visible on the port catapult. The squadron codes on the planes' fuselages are 10-S-13, -14, and -15, representing the thirteenth through fifteenth planes from Cruiser Scouting Squadron 10 (VCS-10). *Special Collections Research Center, Temple University Libraries, Philadelphia*

During the early phase of her service, USS *Indianapolis* was assigned Vought O3U-1 Corsair scout planes. In June 1933, for example, four O3U-1s were serving with the cruiser. In an undated photo probably taken in early 1933 is O3U-1 number 13 from Cruiser Scouting Squadron 10, Bureau Number (BuNo) 8565, bearing the inscription "INDIANAPOLIS" below the squadron code. *National Museum of Naval Aviation*

USS *Indianapolis* made her first transit of the Panama Canal in early March 1933. She is seen here steaming along the canal on the fourth of that month. White awnings are rigged over the forecastle deck and the fantail, to give some relief to the sailors from the tropical sun. The starboard wings of the aircraft, from which the photo was taken, are to the left.

Indianapolis is transiting Gatun Lake, along the Panama Canal, on March 4, 1933. At this time, the ship was painted Standard Navy Gray on all vertical surfaces above the waterline, Standard Deck Gray on steel decks, and natural teak on the wooden decks.

To the left of center, *Indianapolis* is approaching the Pedro Miguel Locks of the Panama Canal on March 4, 1933. Three boats are stacked one atop the other to the starboard side of the boat crane, forward of turret 3.

Indianapolis is steaming through the Culebra Cut, a narrow, mountainous pass in the Panama Canal, on March 4, 1933. The ship's scout planes are not in view. A very close inspection of the photo reveals that an oblong platform has been installed on turret 2, spanning from the center to the left side. This appears to have been for two antiaircraft machine guns, since two pedestals and two boxes, evidently for ammunition, are on the pedestal. The platform was removed by May 1934.

USS *Indianapolis* first visited Honolulu, Hawaii, during a Pacific cruise in April 1933. The cruiser is moored at the pier in the foreground. White awnings have been erected over most of the forecastle and main decks, including the forward turrets. In the left background is the Aloha Tower, a lighthouse. *Naval History and Heritage Command*

Indianapolis is being readied for departure from the Philadelphia Navy Yard following repairs on June 19, 1933. During her period at the yard, ramps and an elevator were installed on the ship to accommodate President Franklin D. Roosevelt; within a few days the cruiser would pick up the physically disabled president at Campobello Island, New Brunswick, and transport him to the US Naval Academy at Annapolis, Maryland. This would be the first of several times *Indianapolis* would transport President Roosevelt. An artist retouched the photo, meticulously inserting the riggings and lines, and the boat crane is lowering a motor whaleboat onto two stacked boats. *Special Collections Research Center, Temple University Libraries, Philadelphia*

O3U-1 number 13 of Cruiser Scouting Squadron 9 is spotted on the well deck of *Indianapolis* around mid-1933. A rudder lock installed over the vertical fin and rudder partially obscures the BuNo, which is 8865. *National Museum of Naval Aviation*

When a cruiser's or battleship's floatplanes were temporarily based on land, the floats were removed and stored, and detachable landing gear were installed. This is the case with these four O3U-1 Corsairs assigned to Cruiser Scouting Squadron 9 and USS *Indianapolis* during a flight on June 12, 1933. *From front to rear,* they bear squadron markings 9-S-13 (and BuNo 8572), 9-S-14 (BuNo 8572), 9-S-15, and 9-S-16. *NARA via Dana Bell*

The same four O3U-1s from VS-9S in the preceding photo are viewed from the left side while flying in formation on June 12, 1933. Especially notable is the narrow fuselage band on 9-S-15. The narrow band indicates that this aircraft was assigned to the assistant commanding officer of the squadron, whereas the broad band of 9-S-13 indicated the commanding officer. *NARA via Dana Bell*

The Scouting Fleet is anchored at Balboa Harbor in the Canal Zone in April 1934. USS *Indianapolis* is the second ship from the right, to the port side of an unidentified battleship. Immediately astern of *Indianapolis* is the Northampton-class cruiser USS *Chicago* (CA-29). *Naval History and Heritage Command*

On May 31, 1934, President Roosevelt was aboard USS *Indianapolis* (*foreground*) in the Atlantic off New York City, to review the fleet. The president is on a reviewing stand to the front of turret 2. The cruiser in the right background is USS *Louisville* (CA-28). In the distance to the upper right, leading the procession of warships to the left is the battleship USS *Pennsylvania* (BB-38).

The presidential flag is flying from the mainmast of *Indianapolis*, and the three-star flag of a US Navy vice admiral is on the foremast during the presidential review of the fleet off New York City on May 31, 1934. A scout plane is on each catapult, and the aircraft crane is in its raised position. *Naval History and Heritage Command*

Small craft are coming in close to *Indianapolis* during FDR's visit to the ship on May 31, 1934. On this occasion, a white cover was lashed down over the top of the forward smokestack; this feature is visible in the several preceding photos. *Naval History and Heritage Command*

Biplanes launched from the carriers *Lexington* (CV-2) and *Saratoga* (CV-3) flew by squadrons in formation over USS *Indianapolis* during President Franklin D. Roosevelt's review of the fleet on May 31, 1934. To the right is USS *Louisville. Naval History and Heritage Command*

President Roosevelt is standing second from left on the reviewing stand on *Indianapolis*. At the top are the forward range clock, below and to the front of which are the forward rangefinder and the distinctive, flared bulwark of the navigating bridge. *Naval History and Heritage Command*

In another close-up photo of the reviewing stand (FDR is in the front row, *third from left*), the tompions in the muzzles of the 8-inch/55-caliber guns are in view. Structural details of the pilothouse and its windows also are in view. *Naval History and Heritage Command*

Members of the crew of *Indianapolis* are manning the rails during the fleet review on May 31, 1934. The reviewing stand for President Roosevelt and other dignitaries is between the rear of turret 1 and the front of turret 2.

The destroyer USS *Sturtevant* (DD-240) is coming alongside *Indianapolis* during the fleet review off New York City on May 31, 1934. The view is from the starboard side of the forward smokestack, facing aft. On the catapult is a Vought Corsair scout plane, to the side of which is the aircraft crane. Searchlights are on the platform on the aft smokestack. *Naval History and Heritage Command*

Indianapolis is viewed from the port side during the May 31, 1934, fleet review. At this time, the roofs of the turrets were painted with a recognition panel with red, white, blue, and yellow squares in a checkerboard pattern. Adjoining light- and dark-colored squares from these devices are visible on all three turret roofs.

Following the fleet review on May 31, 1934, USS *Indianapolis* is silhouetted in the late-afternoon sun as she steams north up New York Harbor, with the Statue of Liberty looming in the background.

Indianapolis enters the Hudson River (also called the North River where it passes to the west of Manhattan) on May 31, 1934, with lower Manhattan in the background and Battery Park to the right. *Naval History and Heritage Command*

With President Franklin D. Roosevelt still aboard, *Indianapolis* passes by skyscrapers on Manhattan's West Side as she proceeds up the Hudson River toward her berth, on May 31, 1934.

Crowds of spectators are visible along the docks and piers as *Indianapolis* cruises past lower Manhattan on May 31, 1934. The Vought Corsair on the port catapult is from Cruiser Scouting Squadron 10 and is marked 10-S-17.

Indianapolis is steaming past a lightly developed area in the area around New York Harbor at the time of the fleet review. The presidential reviewing stand is visible to the front of turret number 2. The red, white, blue, and yellow recognition squares on the turret roofs are visible. *US Navy via A. D. Baker III*

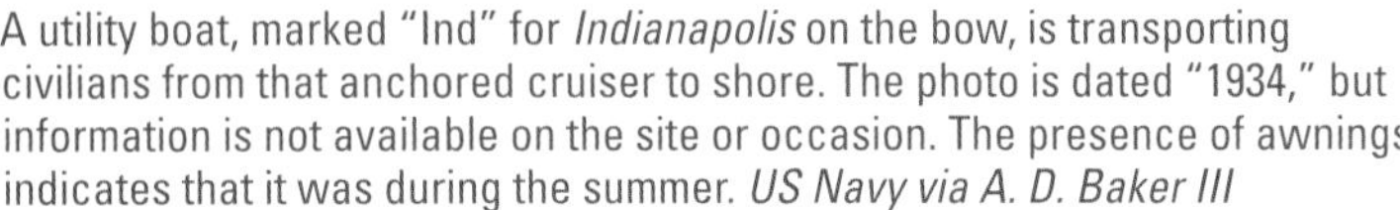

A utility boat, marked "Ind" for *Indianapolis* on the bow, is transporting civilians from that anchored cruiser to shore. The photo is dated "1934," but information is not available on the site or occasion. The presence of awnings indicates that it was during the summer. *US Navy via A. D. Baker III*

USS *Indianapolis* gained a new commanding officer in early 1936: Capt. Henry Kent Hewitt, USN, seen here inspecting the cruiser's Marine detachment as he assumes command on March 16. Also in attendance were the ship's executive officer, Cmdr. Theodore S. Wilkinson, *left*, and 1Lt. John D. Blanchard, USMC. *Naval History and Heritage Command*

USS *Indianapolis* (*left*) and USS *Raleigh* (CL-7), an Omaha-class light cruiser, are moored to Pier 7 at Naval Operating Base (NOB) Norfolk, Virginia, on September 19, 1936. By now, a hood, or cap, had been installed on the front top of the forward smokestack of *Indianapolis*, as a means of deflecting smoke from the foretop. The two aft rangefinders on the navigating bridge have been replaced by two directors for the 5-inch guns; these are believed to have been early-type Mk. 33 directors, with open tops that were covered with canvas tops when not in action. The port director is to the front of the forward smokestack. The forward rangefinder, for navigational use, remained on the front of the navigating bridge.

The cruiser *Indianapolis* is anchored at an unidentified harbor on October 19, 1936. By now, the ship's scout planes were the Curtiss SOC-1, a biplane with two fully enclosed cockpits. Three SOC-1s are visible on the catapults. *US Navy via A. D. Baker III*

President Franklin D. Roosevelt, *fifth from left*, has just come aboard *Indianapolis* at Charleston. To his rear are James Roosevelt, his son and—for this tour—military aide; military aides Capt. Paul H. Bastedo (USN) and Col. E. M. Watson (US Army); and Roosevelt's physician, Capt. Ross T. McIntire (USN). Above them are a Curtiss SOC-1 on the starboard catapult, and, toward the right, the aircraft crane. *Naval History and Heritage Command*

USS *Indianapolis* transported President Franklin D. Roosevelt on a goodwill tour of Latin America in the autumn of 1936. He boarded the ship at Charleston, South Carolina, on November 18. *Indianapolis*'s honor guard and band are shown here rendering honors as President Roosevelt (not in sight) comes aboard the ship at Charleston. The view is facing aft, with the base of the starboard catapult to the left and the band playing to the front of the rolling door of the starboard hangar space in the background. *Naval History and Heritage Command*

Two sailors are holding up the presidential flag in front of the base of the starboard catapult at the time of FDR's South America cruise in late 1936. The flag was the one authorized from 1916 to 1945, with a five-pointed star near each corner. Above the flag are the ship's nameplate, a bell, and a cleat, all three of which are highly polished brass. *Naval History and Heritage Command*

The admiral's cabin, on the port side of the forward superstructure on the forecastle deck of *Indianapolis*, was fitted out as the presidential cabin during Franklin D. Roosevelt's voyage to South America in late 1936. In the foreground is a dining table. An electric fan is on the transverse bulkhead above the bookcase, and two dark curtains are over portholes, the covers of which are raised and secured.

In the forward part of the presidential cabin, normally the admiral's cabin, was the desk and seat used by FDR during his 1936 tour of Latin America. To the lower right of the bookshelf is a clock. A framed painting of a sailing yacht is screwed to the bulkhead.

The "library corner" of the presidential cabin is viewed from next to the dining table. The bookcase is stocked with a variety of books.

President Roosevelt's cabin in *Indianapolis* is viewed from another position, with the dining table in the foreground, the desk in the background, and two portholes with covers open on the outer bulkhead. *Naval History and Heritage Command*

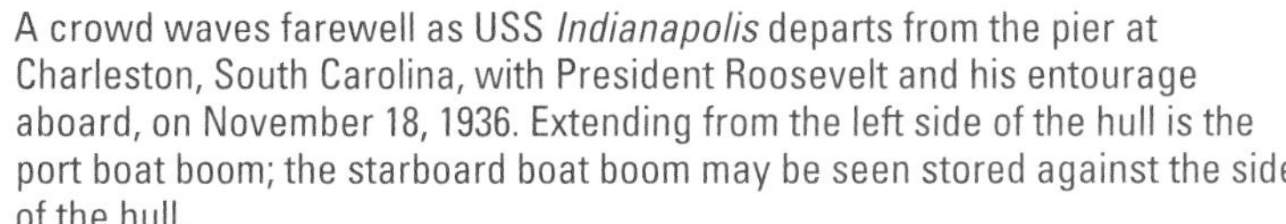

A crowd waves farewell as USS *Indianapolis* departs from the pier at Charleston, South Carolina, with President Roosevelt and his entourage aboard, on November 18, 1936. Extending from the left side of the hull is the port boat boom; the starboard boat boom may be seen stored against the side of the hull.

In the pilothouse of *Indianapolis* during President Roosevelt's goodwill tour of Latin America in late 1936, the helmsman, *second from right*, is steering the ship while two other crewmen attend their duties. The sailor to the left is at the ready behind the engine-order telegraph. The commanding officer of *Indianapolis*, Capt. Henry Kent Hewitt, is seated toward the left center. *Naval History and Heritage Command*

In a view facing forward from a platform on the aft smokestack, two Curtiss VCS-6 SOC-1s are on the catapults, and two more are below, on the main deck, with wings folded. *Naval History and Heritage Command*

When *Indianapolis* crossed the equator on its voyage to South America in November 1936, the crew members who already had "crossed the line" held what is called a Neptune party, or crossing-the-line party. During this event, the veterans of equatorial crossings, called Trusty Shellbacks, hazed and initiated the crewmen who were crossing the line for the first time. Here, Capt. Henry K. Hewitt, commanding officer of *Indianapolis* (*the second officer from left*), transfers his command over to King Neptune at the beginning of the ceremony. *Naval History and Heritage Command*

King Neptune's fierce-looking Royal Police are assembled on the deck of *Indianapolis*, ready to enforce the rules during the equatorial-crossing ceremony. *Naval History and Heritage Command*

President Roosevelt pleads his case before the Royal Court of Shellbacks as his defense attorney listens intently at left, during the Neptune party aboard USS *Indianapolis* as she crosses the equator. The president was excused of the more humiliating aspects of personal attire and behavior the average initiates, called "Pollywogs," were subjected to. *Naval History and Heritage Command*

With President Roosevelt and staff aboard, USS *Indianapolis* made a brief visit to Rio de Janeiro, Brazil, on November 27, 1936. The cruiser is at its dock at Rio, with a Curtiss SOC-1 from Scouting Squadron 11 (VS-11S) on the starboard catapult in the foreground. On the forward end of the catapult are buffers to absorb the shock of the catapult cart upon launching a plane. *Naval History and Heritage Command*

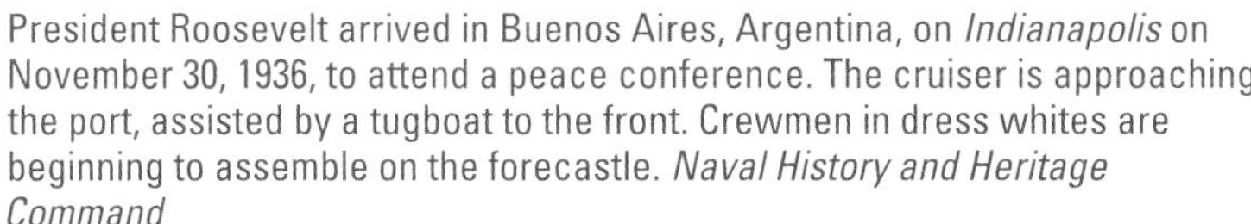

President Roosevelt arrived in Buenos Aires, Argentina, on *Indianapolis* on November 30, 1936, to attend a peace conference. The cruiser is approaching the port, assisted by a tugboat to the front. Crewmen in dress whites are beginning to assemble on the forecastle. *Naval History and Heritage Command*

The Buenos Aires skyline looms ahead as crewmen on the bridge of USS *Indianapolis* take in the novel sights on the cruiser's bridge. Two searchlights are to the right. *Naval History and Heritage Command*

Indianapolis is at the center of the photo, making its way to its berth in the congested harbor. In this photo and the following one, it is clear that the mainmast has been painted black or a dark color. *Naval History and Heritage Command*

Indianapolis is seen entering the harbor of Buenos Aires from a different perspective. On the day after his arrival in that city, Roosevelt delivered an address to the Inter-American Conference for the Maintenance of Peace. The exteriors of the hulls of the ship's boats had been painted a dark color. *US Navy via A. D. Baker III*

Following the conclusion of the peace conference in Buenos Aires, *Indianapolis* began the long journey northward, transporting President Roosevelt back to the United States. First, the ship paid a brief call to Montevideo, Uruguay. The president, in the dark-colored hat and suit to the right, is waving farewell to the people gathered on the dock at Montevideo on December 3, 1936. *Naval History and Heritage Command*

During the voyage north to the United States, *Indianapolis* transited the Panama Canal. In this view from the bridge, the light cruiser USS *Trenton* (CL-11) is approaching on December 6, 1936. In the foreground is the left hood of the rangefinder of turret number 2. *Naval History and Heritage Command*

With President Roosevelt aboard, USS *Indianapolis* made a stop at Port of Spain, Trinidad, to take on fresh supplies on December 11, 1936. Sailors are bringing aboard fresh meat in a cargo net, while others are carrying crates of fresh food. *Naval History and Heritage Command*

Adjacent to the base of one of the catapults, crewmen and officers of USS *Indianapolis* are piping aboard the governor of Trinidad at Port of Spain on December 11, 1936. The governor boarded the ship to pay his respects to President Franklin D. Roosevelt. *Naval History and Heritage Command*

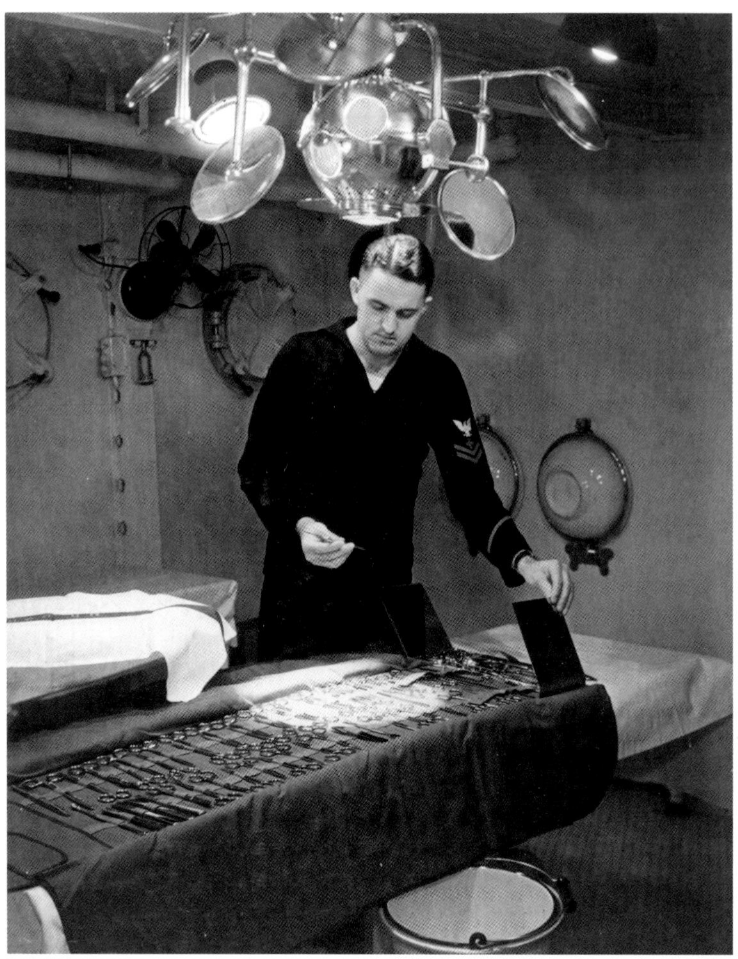

USS *Indianapolis* was equipped with a modern operating room, for the treatment of wounded and sick sailors. Pharmacist Mate 2nd Class Herman H. Barton is arranging surgical instruments in the operating room, with high-intensity operating lights over his head. *Naval History and Heritage Command*

During a visit to Portland, Oregon, for Navy Day in October 1937, *Indianapolis* has just cleared the Burnside Drawbridge, on the Willamette River. The guns of turret number 3 are elevated, and a scout plane is present on the starboard catapult. *Naval History and Heritage Command*

Indianapolis is moored to a dock at the foot of Oak Street in Portland, Oregon, on October 27, 1937. Large white covers have been placed over the 5-inch/25-caliber dual-purpose guns abeam and aft of the aft smokestack. *Naval History and Heritage Command*

Crewmen on the fantail of the New Orleans–class cruiser USS *Minneapolis* (CA-36) are hauling on a hawser from their ship to USS *Indianapolis* for purposes of mooring the two ships together at sea, sometime during 1937. Before this time, the mainmast of *Indianapolis* had been repainted from a dark color to a light gray. *US Navy via A. D. Baker III*

Indianapolis is proceeding at low speed in Pearl Harbor during a deployment to the Pacific in 1937. Sometimes during transit, the scout planes were doubled up on the catapults. Such is the case here; two Curtiss SOC-1s are mounted on the port catapult. *Naval History and Heritage Command*

The port side of USS *Indianapolis* is observed from the air in a high-contrast photo dated March 29, 1939. The four-colored, checkerboard recognition panels on the turret roofs of several years earlier had been replaced by a new system: rectangles on the roofs of turrets 1 and 2 and a circle on turret 3, painted in the color of the scouting squadron then assigned to the ship. In the case of *Indianapolis*, this color was either black or green, depending on the date. When this photo was taken, her aircraft were in section 4, so the circle would have been black.

The following sequence of photographs was taken in New York City during a naval review in June 1939. The ship was painted overall in #5 Standard Navy Gray above the boot topping except for #20 Deck Gray on the metal decks.

Indianapolis is viewed from closer to the bow. Prominent on the wing of the navigating bridge, on the level above the pilothouse, is the port secondary-battery director, with a rangefinder and a canvas cover over the open top. An identical director is on the starboard wing. On the front of the navigating bridge is a navigational rangefinder. At the summit of the foretop is the Mk. 27 primary-battery director. The directors were manned by crewmen who visually acquired and tracked targets and controlled the firing of the guns. *Naval History and Heritage Command*

The forward superstructure of *Indianapolis* in 1939 was virtually the same as its state when commissioned. A dark-colored boat boom is in the stored position on the side of the hull. A gun for firing salutes is on the first level above the forecastle deck, inboard of the forward boat davit. This level was referred to as the communication platform. An "E"-for-efficiency award is on the side of turret 2. *Naval History and Heritage Command*

The cruiser is viewed from the front at New York in June 1939. A very close view of the photo reveals that canvas sleeves have been secured over the tubes of the rangefinder. *Naval History and Heritage Command*

Indianapolis is viewed from the pier she is moored to in New York in June 1939. The boats on the davits to each side of the superstructure are painted a light color above the waterline, and dark on the gunwale and the hull below the waterline. "Ind." was painted on the bow in a dark color. *Naval History and Heritage Command*

In a photo of *Indianapolis* during a visit to New York City in or around June 1939, a barge is moored to the boat boom. A boarding ladder has been rigged, leading up to the main deck below the starboard catapult. A clear view is available of the white canvas covers over the 5-inch/25-caliber gun mounts. *Naval History and Heritage Command*

USS *Indianapolis* is at sea in a photograph dated September 27, 1939. The rectangular recognition panels on the roof of the turret are clearly visible. On the sides of each of the turrets are two crew doors and, just aft of the forward door, ladder rungs for accessing the roof.

In a rare prewar color photo, USS *Indianapolis* is anchored in Hawaiian waters during maneuvers in September 1940. The ship was painted overall in #5 Standard Navy Gray, with black smokestack caps, and natural-wood decks. The boat booms, of which four are visible, have a tan or brown color, apparently representing a wood preservative. Black rectangles painted in the ship's scouting squadron (VCS-6) color are on the roofs of turrets 1 and 2, while a 12-foot Willow Green dot was atop turret 3, representing section 5. *Carl Mydans, Getty Images*

CHAPTER 2

Pearl Harbor to Okinawa

On the fateful morning of December 7, 1941, *Indianapolis* was 710 miles away as part of the six-ship Task Force 3, conducting a gunnery exercise at Johnston Atoll. She was immediately reassigned to Task Force 12 and sortied in search of the Japanese carriers. *Indianapolis* entered a smoky, oil-covered Pearl Harbor on December 13 and was returned to Task Force 11. She sailed the next day as part of a diversion for the ultimately aborted effort by Task Force 14 under Frank Jack Fletcher to relieve Wake Island.

Indianapolis and Task Force 11 ultimately made contact with the enemy about 350 miles south of Rabaul, New Britain, on the afternoon of February 20, 1942.

The task force, centered on USS *Lexington* (CV-2), came under attack from eighteen Japanese twin-engined bombers. The Americans shot down sixteen of the enemy aircraft, with none of the US vessels suffering any damage.

Reinforced with the addition of the carrier *Yorktown* (CV-5), on March 10, 1942, the Task Force 11 aircraft attacked enemy positions at Lae and Salamaua, New Guinea. Japanese aircraft rose to strike back, but *Indianapolis* was unscathed.

The cruiser then steamed for Mare Island for overhaul and alterations, including notable improvements in her antiaircraft batteries. This work was completed in April 1942. Upon departure from the West Coast, *Indianapolis* escorted a convoy to Australia, arriving at Port Melbourne on May 13. She left three days later, steaming for Pearl Harbor. After a refueling stop in Pago Pago on May 22, she arrived at Pearl Harbor on May 27. She left the warm Hawaiian waters two days later, steaming for the North Pacific to counterattack the Japanese who had landed in the barren, inhospitable Aleutian Islands. The next day *Indianapolis* rendezvoused with Task Group 8.6, steaming for Kodiak, where they arrived on June 8. *Indianapolis* became the flagship of Task Force 8.

The Japanese 301st Independent Infantry Battalion had landed on Attu Island on June 7, 1942, and taken the undefended island, which is 1,100 miles from mainland Alaska. Concerned that the Japanese had a strategically located outpost, the US first cut off Japanese supply efforts for Attu and Kiska.

On July 2, while *Indianapolis* was on routine patrol, her plane 4-CS-15 crashed and sank, taking with it pilot Lt. (jg) W. B. Billings and Aircraft Radioman First Class William Kyde. On July 11, while moored at Kodiak, Capt. E. W. Hanson was relieved by Capt. Morton Deyo. Capt. Deyo had been in command for only nine days when, during an underway refueling of the destroyer *Elliot* (DD-146), Seaman 2nd class R. R. Hogan fell overboard from *Indianapolis*. *Elliot* cast loose from *Indianapolis* and sought to recover the man, succeeding just over an hour later. Unfortunately, the harsh Alaskan waters were too cold, and the seaman could not be revived. *Elliot*'s doctor reported he had succumbed to exposure. Hogan's body was returned to the *Indianapolis*, where later that day Deyo officiated at a burial-at-sea service.

On August 3, *Indianapolis* got underway from Naval Air Station Kodiak, bound for Kiska, which was targeted for bombardment. She opened fire on enemy installations there with her main battery at 0601 on August 7. When she ceased firing sixteen minutes later, 360 rounds of 8-inch ammunition had been hurled at the enemy. She returned to Naval Air Station Kodiak on August 11.

On September 28, 1942, while the ship was on routine patrol, *Indianapolis*'s aircraft 4-CS-13 was severely damaged during landing, requiring the crew to be rescued by *Indianapolis*, with the severely damaged aircraft being recovered as well.

Indianapolis continued a routine of daily patrols, training exercises, and general support in Alaskan waters until November

USS *Indianapolis* visited Mare Island Naval Shipyard, Vallejo, California, in the spring of 1942 for refitting and modernization. During that period in the yard, the ship's armaments were upgraded. Two single 20 mm guns on pedestal mounts, seen in this April 18, 1942, photo with canvas covers, were installed on the forecastle deck. A splinter shield around the gun mount provided the crew with some protection from shrapnel during battle. Two ladder rungs on the shields provided access to their interiors.

16, when she left Kuluk Bay, Adak Island, bound for Pearl Harbor. She arrived on November 22 and the next day entered the Navy yard for repairs and improvements. While in the Navy yard, Capt. Deyo was relieved by Capt. Nicholas Vytlacil. The shipyard work was completed on December 14, and the ship left Pearl Harbor for refresher training and drills. She returned to the Navy yard for further repairs on December 16 and remained there until that work was completed on December 22.

During her time in Pearl Harbor, her TBA, TBB, TAJ, TAU, TAQ, TBF, and CSB and her two RAA transmitters were removed and replaced with TBM, TBU, TBA-6, and TBK-12 equipment. Her SC radar was replaced by SA radar, and SG, BL, FC, and two FD systems were installed.

Also, two quadruple 40 mm mounts were installed on the main deck aft along with corresponding Mk. 51 directors, magazines, sprinklers, clipping rooms, and splinter shields. Four 1.1-inch mounts were exchanged for new mounts with electric drive and Mk. 51 directors installed for those mounts. The 20 mm battery was rearranged, and seven new guns were added, bringing the total to nineteen.

Her boat crane was removed, and the conning tower was altered for use as primary ship control station. Various combustibles were removed from the ship, including cork insulation, tiling, and the wood from the quarterdeck. The ship was also painted below the waterline.

She left Pearl Harbor on December 22 and arrived in Dutch Harbor, Alaska, on December 28, 1942.

On January 12, 1943, *Indianapolis* supported the unopposed US Army landing on Amchitka, in the Aleutians, where an Army airfield would be built.

On February 18, along with *Richmond* (CL-9), *Bancroft* (DD-598), *Caldwell* (DD-605), *Coghlan* (DD-606), and *Gillespie* (DD-609), *Indianapolis* approached Attu, and at 1504 hours *Indianapolis*'s main and secondary batteries began firing on enemy positions on the island. She fired first at 13,500 yards and then at 15,150 yards. *Indianapolis* fired 174 rounds of 5"/25 ammunition, eighty-four rounds of 8-inch high-capacity ammunition, and twenty-nine rounds of 8-inch armor-piercing (AP) ammunition. The latter was fired, one round per salvo, because the AP ammunition had

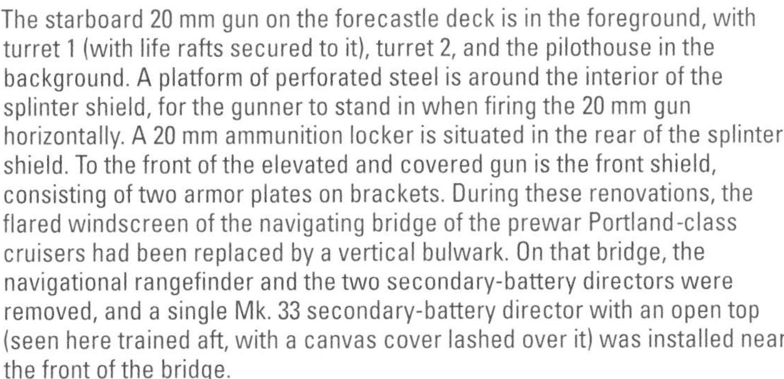

The starboard 20 mm gun on the forecastle deck is in the foreground, with turret 1 (with life rafts secured to it), turret 2, and the pilothouse in the background. A platform of perforated steel is around the interior of the splinter shield, for the gunner to stand in when firing the 20 mm gun horizontally. A 20 mm ammunition locker is situated in the rear of the splinter shield. To the front of the elevated and covered gun is the front shield, consisting of two armor plates on brackets. During these renovations, the flared windscreen of the navigating bridge of the prewar Portland-class cruisers had been replaced by a vertical bulwark. On that bridge, the navigational rangefinder and the two secondary-battery directors were removed, and a single Mk. 33 secondary-battery director with an open top (seen here trained aft, with a canvas cover lashed over it) was installed near the front of the bridge.

With the installation of 20 mm guns at various places on *Indianapolis* at Mare Island, it was necessary to provide clipping rooms, where the magazines for the guns were reloaded. The drum-shaped magazines had a capacity of sixty rounds. This clipping room is on the starboard side of superstructure on the forecastle deck, aft of the captain's cabin; storage racks are visible inside.

red dye, allowing *Indianapolis*'s shell fall to be distinguished from *Richmond*'s, which was adjacent.

Just before midnight on February 19, 1943, while *Indianapolis* along with destroyers *Coghlan* (DD-606) and *Gillespie* (DD-609) patrolled southwest of Attu, they intercepted an unknown ship. When challenged, the vessel sent a reply in Japanese code and was thus identified as an enemy vessel. *Indianapolis* fired a salvo of 8-inch rounds, striking the vessel, later identified as the 3,121-ton cargo ship *Akagane Maru*, setting the ship afire from stem to stern. The Japanese vessel went under at 0126 on February 20, with no survivors.

Retiring to Dutch Harbor on February 24, she remained in port until Thursday, March 4, when she got underway for San Francisco, passing beneath the Golden Gate Bridge on March 9. The next day the crew began unloading the ammunition from the ship prior to her entering Mare Island Navy Yard. During the continued unloading operations the next day, Seaman 2nd Class Frederick Dempsey fell overboard at 1223. Coxswain J. E. Herbert dove in to save him but could not find the man. At 1250 the body of Dempsey was recovered, but despite twenty minutes of CPR, he could not be revived.

On Tuesday, March 16, *Indianapolis* entered the drydock in Mare Island shipyard for overhaul and refit, during which time a new mainmast was installed and the bridge was cut down, and additional 20 mm and 40 mm antiaircraft guns were installed. This gave her a mixed antiaircraft battery of 20 mm, 40 mm, and 1.1-inch antiaircraft guns, and 5"/25 dual-purpose guns. A new deckhouse housing secondary steering was built around the aft funnel.

She left drydock on Tuesday, April 27, and tied up at berth 22-S in the yard. Although occasionally shifting berths, she remained at Mare Island until May 2, taking on fuel and ammunition. On that day she steamed to San Francisco Bay, dropping anchor off Hunters Point. The next couple of days were spent testing various systems, and on May 4 she conducted a full-power run off California, attaining 32.5 knots. Ten minutes after this run, at 1355, nine men were washed overboard. *Indianapolis* circled back to pick up the men, and a blimp overhead dropped a life float. *Indianapolis* found three men, recovering two, while the third was struck by the propeller guard as the ship drifted by, engines at stop. The third man was forced underwater and could not be found. Despite continued searching, none of the other men were found. The crew was mustered to quarters, and thus the men lost overboard were identified as W. M. Donovan, L. P. O'Brien, L. Roble, H. J. Fox, J. J. Legendre, R. E. Lee, and G. Mayea. Ultimately, the search was suspended, and the ship returned to Mare Island.

She left Mare Island on May 7, arriving at North Island, San Diego, on May 12. After a brief return to San Francisco, she steamed north, returning to Alaskan waters on May 24, 1943.

Although operations began to retake Attu in May 1943, *Indianapolis* did not take part in this. Similarly, when Kiska was subjected to naval bombardment from August 2 through August 14, *Indianapolis* did not take part. While Attu was the sight of bloody land battles (with the naval artillery aiding US troops ashore), under the cover of bad weather the Japanese had evacuated Kiska before the 34,426 invading US troops landed on August 15.

On August 24, 1943, *Indianapolis* left Kuluk Bay, Adak Island, steaming for San Francisco Bay, which she reached on August 31. On September 4 her ammunition stores were replenished, and on September 7 she began steaming toward Pearl Harbor, reaching that anchorage on September 11, 1943.

On Friday, November 5, *Indianapolis* became the flagship for VAdm. Raymond Spruance, commander of the Central Pacific Force (redesignated the Fifth Fleet on April 26, 1944). *Indianapolis* sailed from Pearl Harbor at 0820 on November 10 with the main body of the Southern Attack Force of the Assault Force for Operation Galvanic, the invasion of the Gilbert Islands. *Indianapolis*'s crew was well prepared, with the SECRET Special Action report noting, "All possible advantage was taken of reconnaissance photographs of the Atoll to train spotters, director operators, radar operators, C.I.C. team[,] and navigation team in the identification of prominent land-marks and target areas. Schools were organized for this purpose[,] and study conducted daily from the time of departure from Pearl Harbor. Photographs of the Atoll taken by the *Nautilus* were of the greatest value for this purpose."

On November 17, 1943, *Indianapolis* steamed from Pearl Harbor as part of a force of cruisers taking part in Operation Galvanic, the invasion of Tarawa. *Indianapolis* began shore bombardment at 1804 on November 20, with her 8-inch rifles firing at 22,000 yards. The initial target, observation tower number 1, was engaged by indirect fire. The crew experienced difficulty with indirect fire, with the report noting, "apparently due to incorrect initial bearings and too rapidly changing parallex at close range."

The other four targets during this phase were engaged with direct fire, with a total of ninety rounds of 5"/25 common and 179 rounds of 8"/55 high-capacity rounds being expended.

At 1950 *Indianapolis* was called upon to destroy a Japanese shore battery of heavy guns at the eastern tip of Bititu Island. She trained her 8-inch guns on the target and, firing in three-gun salvos, except for the second salvo, which was a full nine-gun salvo, in short order destroyed the enemy position. Later survey

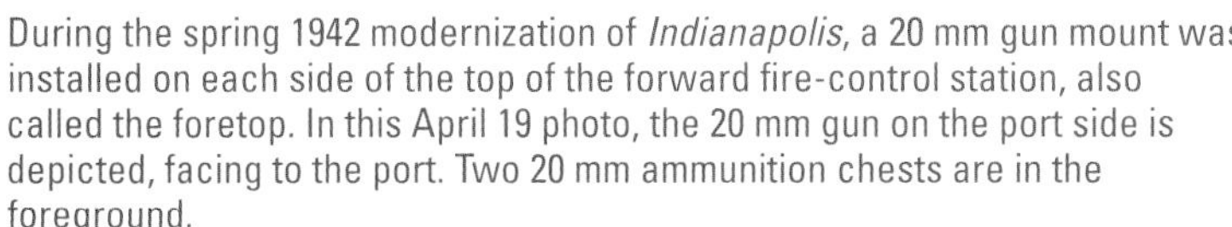

During the spring 1942 modernization of *Indianapolis*, a 20 mm gun mount was installed on each side of the top of the forward fire-control station, also called the foretop. In this April 19 photo, the 20 mm gun on the port side is depicted, facing to the port. Two 20 mm ammunition chests are in the foreground.

Two 20 mm gun mounts were placed on the sides of the navigating bridge. The starboard one is seen from above on April 18, 1942; the foredeck is visible below. Visible here are sections of curved floor and bulwark to accommodate the 20 mm guns, and a curved platform for the gunner.

revealed that at least one of the enemy 8-inch guns was trained toward the position *Indianapolis* was firing from.

Phase 2 of the bombardment began at 2024 and lasted almost ten minutes. During this time, 256 further rounds of 5"/25 and eighty-one rounds of 8"/55 were expended.

On November 22 her 5-inch guns were called for by troops ashore to take aim at a target at the eastern end of Bititu Island, with the report noting, "No difficulty was experienced in getting on the targets at 7,000 yards, but difficulty was experienced in staying on by reason of the ship drifting while the engines were stopped."

Indianapolis stayed in the immediate vicinity of Tarawa, screening other ships and the island, through December 7. On December 6, she received from the Marines eight Japanese POWs for transport to Pearl Harbor, for which she departed the following morning. *Indianapolis* arrived at Pearl Harbor on December 11, and the next day Adm. Spruance transferred his command ashore.

On December 13, *Indianapolis* detached twelve officers and 366 for temporary duty and received fifty-two officers and 646 enlisted as passengers for transit to San Francisco, for which she left immediately, arriving December 18 and discharging her passengers.

Dawn on New Year's Day saw *Indianapolis* moored at the Mare Island Navy Yard, ending her restricted availability. At 0717 she got underway, moving to San Francisco, where the next day she took on board ninety-nine officers and 965 enlisted men for transport to Pearl Harbor.

Indianapolis arrived at Pearl Harbor on January 7, 1944. She remained there until January 11, when she began conducting daily gunnery exercises through January 13. On January 15 she entered Pearl Harbor Navy Yard for a limited availability. On January 18, with the shipyard work complete, VAdm. Spruance returned aboard and *Indianapolis*, flagship of the Central Pacific Force, left Pearl Harbor on January 19, rendezvousing with the rest of the Southern Attack Force at Tarawa before steaming to Kwajalein Atoll, the target of the first phase of Operation Flintlock. It appears that during the time the ship was at Pearl, an exhaust deflector was added to the aft funnel. On the twenty-sixth they joined with Carrier Task Group 58.2 and remained until she detached at 0814 on the thirty-first and proceeded independently, without escort, to join Task Unit 53.5.2 off Roi at dawn on the thirtieth.

Analysis of Tarawa had shown that bombardments needed to be longer and better coordinated, and that improvements in ammunition choice needed to be made. All these lessons were incorporated into the bombardment of Kwajalein, which began on the thirtieth.

The landings began on January 31, with the main landings on Roi and Namur taking place on the morning of February 1. During this time *Indianapolis* knocked out two shore batteries, a blockhouse, and other enemy targets. Notably, she supported advancing troops with a creeping barrage, a lesson learned at Tarawa. On D-plus-2 day, *Indianapolis* dropped anchor in Kwajalein Lagoon. On February 8 she moved to Majuro, where the fast carrier force was anchored.

On February 15, *Indianapolis* steamed from Kwajalein Atoll as part of Task Group 51.11, bound for Eniwetok as part of Operation Catchpole. February 17 had been designated as Dog Day, or D-day, for the invasion. She was assigned to Fire Support Section 3, which also included her sister ship, *Portland*, as well as two destroyers. At 0700 on February 17, *Indianapolis*'s main battery opened fire at targets on Eniwetok, continuing the pounding until 0850, at which time aviators took over until 0859, when *Indianapolis*'s 8-inch rifles resumed firing. The cruiser recorded direct hits on three pillboxes.

At 1246 she shot her way into the lagoon via the deep entrance, with *Indianapolis* firing 190 rounds of 40 mm ammunition at boats on the beaches of Parry Island. At 1554, *Indianapolis* was advised that minesweepers had cleared fire support area 9, and got under way for that area. At 1619 her main battery began firing at targets on Eniwetok, at ranges of 3,000 to 5,000 yards, scoring several hits.

After spending the night at anchor, at 0713 *Indianapolis* again got underway and at 0747 began harassing fire throughout the day.

Similarly, on February 19, *Indianapolis* got underway at 0614 and took up her position in the southern part of fire support area 9, anchoring there and firing upon assigned targets, as well as targets of opportunity. A combination of 8-inch, 5-inch, and 40 mm weapons were used.

Similar operations took place over the next couple of days, and at 2200 on February 22, star shell illumination of Parry by *Indianapolis* was ordered, which continued until 0107 the next morning. During this operation it was learned that a considerable number of the 241 star shells fired were duds.

Indianapolis fired 341 8-inch and 617 5-inch rounds on Parry Island, and 540 8-inch and 169 5-inch rounds at Eniwetok. During these operations, *Indianapolis* and *Portland* had been designated as refueling and rearming stations for all seaplanes in the operation, over the course of which she serviced forty-nine airplanes, using 6,000 gallons of gasoline.

On March 16, *Louisville* (CA-28) transferred 190 rounds of 5"/25 star shells to *Indianapolis*, to augment the forty-one rounds that remained from the firing in February. At 0900 on March 22, 1944, *Indianapolis* steamed from Majuro Lagoon as part of Task Unit 58.9.2. At noon on March 27, 1944, *Indianapolis* along with the other cruisers separated to form Task Unit 58.3.13 under RAdm. J. B. Oldendorf aboard *Louisville*. The vessels formed part of the screen for carrier strikes on the Palau Islands on March 30–31, Yap and Ulithi on the thirty-first, and Woleai on April 1. During this time, *Indianapolis*'s gunners downed an enemy torpedo bomber.

On April 10, Adm. Spruance shifted his flag from *New Jersey* (BB-62) back to *Indianapolis* and left Majuro for Pearl Harbor, arriving April 14.

On April 16, after taking on numerous passengers, she steamed for San Francisco, arriving on April 21. While *Indianapolis* was moored in San Francisco Bay, on April 26, 1944, the Central Pacific Force was redesignated the Fifth Fleet, with Adm. Spruance in command. The next three days were spent replenishing stores and ammunition and taking aboard passengers bound for Hawaii.

The ship's war diary noted the following on April 30: "Completed application of Camouflage Design 7D to outward surfaces of the ship." That pattern consisted of Light Gray (5-L), Ocean Gray (5-O), and Black (BK) applied in what is commonly called a dazzle pattern. Counter to what some other published sources state, the ship's logs indicate that she was not refitted or repaired during

Aft of the aft smokestack was the searchlight-control platform. During the work at Mare Island in early 1942, a 20 mm gun mount and splinter shield were installed on each side of that platform. In a view of the port mount, facing aft, a 20 mm ammunition locker is to the left; above it is the aft rangefinder.

A 20 mm ammunition clipping room was established on the port side of the communication platform (i.e., the 01 level: the first level above the forecastle deck) during the modernizations in early 1942, as seen in an April 18 photo. The compartment was several yards to the port of the front of the forward smokestack. The view is facing forward.

Another 20 mm clipping room was built on the port side of the deck over the hangars, as seen in an April 18, 1942, photo at Mare Island. Elbow vents were installed on these clipping rooms.

This 20 mm clipping room was installed on the navigating bridge. To the sides of the compartment are the aft struts of the tripod foremast.

this time. On May 1 she left San Francisco, steaming independently to Pearl Harbor and arriving on May 6. The following twenty days were filled with occasional voyages in Hawaiian waters for training, and considerable time tied up in Pearl Harbor.

On May 26, *Indianapolis* left Pearl Harbor with Adm. Spruance aboard, bound for Majuro, arriving on June 2 (local time). On June 5 she steamed the short distance to Roi, allowing Spruance to inspect installations on Roi and Namur, and the next day left for Eniwetok, arriving on June 7 for a similar inspection. *Indianapolis*, with Spruance aboard and escorted by *Stanly* (DD-478), left that anchorage on June 9 for a rendezvous with TF58. *Indianapolis* and the task force made their way for the Marianas. The task force's carriers launched airstrikes beginning on June 11, and on June 13 *Indianapolis* arrived off Saipan and Tinian, while other ships

A gallery of two 20 mm guns was established on the fantail of *Indianapolis* during the modernizations at Mare Island, as shown in a photo dated April 18, 1942. A splinter shield with an entrance on the front was installed, as well as 20 mm ammunition lockers. The shield had flanges at intervals on the bottom, which were bolted to the deck. There was room on each side of the splinter shield for crewmen to pass back and forth. Two depth-charge racks now were present on the rear of the fantail, and they are partially visible.

Indianapolis is viewed from amidships to the bow at Mare Island on April 19, 1942. During this modernization, a Mk. 3 fire-control radar antenna had been mounted atop the forward Mk. 27 main-battery director, at the top of the photo to the front of the foremast. The two aft rangefinders and the wings they were installed on had been removed from the rear of the navigating bridge. A quadruple 1.1-inch gun mount had been installed on a platform on each side of the 01 level, adjacent to the superstructure, and to the front of each of these mounts were a 20 mm gun and splinter shield.

At Mare Island in April 1942, two Curtiss SOC-1s from Cruiser Scouting Squadron 4 (VCS-4) are on the catapults, and a third one is below, on the main deck. The plane on the port catapult is marked "4-CS-15," and the plane number, 15, is marked on the upper wing.

This photo continues aft from the preceding one, showing *Indianapolis* from the aft smokestack to the fantail. Details of the aircraft crane are shown, including its king post, from which two braces run down through the searchlight platform to the 01 level. Between the second and third 5-inch/25-caliber gun mounts is a quadruple 1.1-inch gun mount.

shelled shore installations; the war diary of ComFifthFleet specifically states, "INDIANAPOLIS did not bombard." On June 14, *Indianapolis* was part of Bombardment Group 1 northwest of Saipan, shelling positions thereon. She also was one of three US ships to each be hit by single Japanese 4.7" rounds that day. The war diary noted that the damage to *Indianapolis* "was inconsequential."

June 18 found *Indianapolis* operating with Task Groups 58.2, 58.3, and 58.7 west of Saipan, poised to combat the Japanese fleet that was coming in hopes of repelling the US landings in the Marianas.

While the surface fleets did not clash, carrier-borne aircraft certainly did, with the next day coming to be known as the Great Marianas Turkey Shoot. *Indianapolis*'s antiaircraft gunners were involved, even if the big guns were not, and downed a Japanese torpedo bomber.

Following the air clash, *Indianapolis* joined Task Group 58.8 in pursuit of the retreating Japanese, in hopes of sinking stragglers. However, an easterly wind, low fuel levels of the destroyers, and the necessity of recovering many downed fliers severely hampered this progress. Thus, at 2000 on June 21, pursuit of the Japanese was discontinued and *Indianapolis* began to retire toward Saipan, 700 miles behind.

Indianapolis anchored off Saipan at 1245 on June 23. There, on June 25 she was assigned to Cruiser Division 4 and covered the night retirement of transports. *Indianapolis* continued operations against Saipan until June 29, with the war diary noting, "INDIANAPOLIS returned to SAIPAN anchorage after daylight and fueled from SUAMICO. In the afternoon, INDIANAPOLIS conducted bombardment of TINIAN town and vicinity."

The next day, the diary observes, "INDIANAPOLIS returned to the vicinity of SAIPAN after daylight and conducted bombardment on shore targets in the vicinity of MUCHO Point throughout the day."

July 20 found *Indianapolis* shelling Guam, part of one of the most prolonged preinvasion bombardments ever. The III Amphibious Corps landed on Guam the morning of July 21. *Indianapolis* continued this landing until July 23, when she shifted her sights to Tinian, the target of landings the next day.

On the afternoon of July 29, *Indianapolis*, with Spruance aboard, dropped anchor in Apra Harbor, Guam. She weighed anchor and made her way unescorted for Saipan at 1900 hours, arriving the next morning and anchoring off western Saipan. She would remain there until 1800 on August 9, when she steamed for Guam, returning to Apra Harbor at 1030 on August 10. She weighed anchor at 1800 on August 13, steaming to Tanapag Harbor, Saipan, and arriving the next morning. A week later, at 0700 on August 20, she steamed for Tinian, anchoring off Tinian town, remaining until August 22, when she sailed for Eniwetok. She anchored in Eniwetok lagoon at 1600 on August 24, remaining there until 0830 on August 27, when she steamed unescorted for Kwajalein, arriving the next morning.

There, by order of Adm. Nimitz, Spruance turned over responsibility for the forward area to Adm. Halsey, and along with it, all Fifth Fleet forces except *Indianapolis*. At 1000 hours, Spruance and *Indianapolis* sailed for Pearl Harbor, arriving on September 1. Upon arrival, Adm. Spruance transferred his flag to a shore base. On September 2, *Indianapolis* too became part of Third Fleet and left Pearl Harbor at 1809 hours, her crew having enjoyed a brief liberty.

From September 12 through 29, she bombarded the island of Peleliu in the Palau group, both before and after the landings, withdrawing only briefly to refuel from the battleship *Mississippi* (BB-41) on September 19 and replenish ammunition at sea the next day.

On October 1, she sailed with three other cruisers and several smaller ships to Seeadler Harbor, Manus, in the Admiralty Islands. She left that anchorage on October 4, bound for Pearl Harbor, along with another cruiser and two battleships, arriving on October 14. About three and a half hours later, having taken on 336,854 gallons of bunker fuel, she set out without escort for Mare Island Navy Yard for overhaul, arriving on October 19. The next day, all ammunition and the remaining fuel were unloaded. Work began on *Indianapolis* while she was moored at berth 22, and on November 14 she was moved into drydock number 2. It was there, on November 18, that Capt. Charles B. McVay III relieved Capt. Einar Johnson in command. *Indianapolis* left drydock on November 26 at 1058. On December 2, McVay took the *Indianapolis* to sea for her postrepair trials. The next day the ship anchored at berth 25, San Francisco Bay. She returned to Mare Island on December 5 for further work and reentered drydock number 2 on December 8, leaving the next day. Repairs completed, on December 11 she steamed for San Diego. During the following days of routine drills and exercises, a serious defect was discovered in the control valves of the main turbines, and the captain decided to return to port for emergency repair, tying up at Pier 3, Naval Repair Base, San Diego, on December 16. Repairs completed, *Indianapolis* put to sea on December 19 and resumed training.

Finally, on January 3 she steamed for Pearl Harbor in the company of other vessels, reaching that installation on January 9. On January 13, Adm. Spruance returned aboard, again making the *Indianapolis* his flagship. The next morning she put to sea, bound for Saipan, but those orders were altered on January 23, with the new destination being Ulithi, where *Indianapolis* arrived on January

Indianapolis is underway following her period at Mare Island Naval Shipyard on April 20, 1942. As part of that work, the ship received a new camouflage paint scheme, Measure 21, consisting of Navy Blue (5-N) on all horizontal surfaces above the waterline and Deck Blue (20-B) on the decks and horizontal surfaces. The ship's number, 35, was painted in relatively small numerals on the bow. During this refitting, the portholes on the hull, except for those above the main deck, were removed and plated over, since it had been found that portholes would hasten the sinking of a ship.

In the World War II US Navy, African Americans were relegated to duty as mess attendants and stewards, but they also were allowed to volunteer for additional duty in positions that exposed them to combat. These members of the crew of USS *Indianapolis*, photographed in July 1942, volunteered to serve on gun crews. The cruiser's commanding officer, Capt. E. W. Hanson, is second from the right.

As part of Task Force 8, *Indianapolis* participated in the US attack on Japanese occupiers of Kiska Island, in the Aleutians, in early August 1942. On the seventh of the month, a Japanese fighter caused this damage to the wing of one of *Indianapolis*'s Curtiss SOC Seagull scout planes. The photo was taken after the plane was recovered and hoisted onto the main deck.

25. While anchored there, on February 2, Adm. Chester Nimitz came aboard, the first five-star flag officer to break his flag aboard *Indianapolis*. The next day, about forty flag officers were aboard for a conference with Nimitz, and he departed on February 4.

Indianapolis joined VAdm. Marc A. Mitscher's fast carrier Task Force 58 on February 14, 1945, and two days later the task force's aircraft struck Tokyo. On the eighteenth, *Indianapolis* along with two other cruisers and two fast battleships was detached to proceed to Iwo Jima. On February 20, *Indianapolis* was used for special fire support missions off Iwo. These missions included pre–King Hour bombardment, then shifted to counterbattery, targets of opportunity, and deep-support targets. On the night of March 2, she was again assigned to special missions, delivering harassing fire on the enemy. On March 3–4, *Indianapolis* was utilized on daytime direct-support assignments, a responsibility that carried through the night of March 4 and through the day of March 5, when she steamed unescorted for Ulithi, arriving on March 9.

On March 14, *Indianapolis,* as part of the screen for the fast carrier force, departed Ulithi and steamed for the coast of Japan. About 100 miles southeast of Kyushu on March 18, the US carriers launched their airplanes against airfields on the island, and ships of the Japanese fleet in the harbors of Kobe and Kure on southern Honshu.

On March 24, *Indianapolis*, along with *Washington* (BB-56) and *South Dakota* (BB-57), and four destroyers were detached from Task Group 58.3 and steamed to rendezvous with Adm. Lee's fast battleships (Task Group 59.7), which they would join to bombard southern Okinawa. However, because mines had not been swept close to shore, the bombardment was undertaken by the battleships at ranges greater than the *Indy*'s 8-inch gun could fire. *Indianapolis* maneuvered with the force and undertook training.

By March 26, mines had been swept and *Indianapolis*, now a part of the Tonachi Fire Support Unit, could close range enough to fire ten rounds of 8"/55 ammunition at enemy boats seen along the shore of Tonachi town.

On the next day, *Indianapolis* as well as her escorting ships came under Japanese air attack. *Indianapolis*'s gunners aided in bringing down two of the enemy aircraft, one crashing close aboard the port bow. Fighting off these aircraft, *Indianapolis*'s gunners expended thirty-six 5-inch rounds, 510 rounds of 40 mm, and 970 rounds of 20 mm ammunition.

On March 28, *Indianapolis* expended a further fifty-nine rounds of 8-inch ammunition shelling positions on Okinawa. On the next day, thanks to effective minesweeping, she was able to close range to 2,000–3,000 yards of shore and thus deliver more-effective fire, including 171 8-inch rounds and ninety-three rounds of 40 mm, which was very effective at removing jungle growth.

Indianapolis is anchored off Adak, in the Aleutians, in October 1942. The aircraft crane is towering to the front of the aft smokestack, and a boarding ladder is rigged amidships, for access to the well deck. *US Naval Institute / Alfred J. Sedivi Collection*

In a photo of *Indianapolis* anchored in Cold Bay, in the Aleutians, in October 1942, the depth-charge racks that were installed at Mare Island earlier that year are protruding over the stern. Although not easily visible, on the outboard sides of those racks are smoke generators, for laying down smokescreens. Stacked life rafts are on the sides and the roofs of the turrets and on the decks. *Naval History and Heritage Command*

Indianapolis received further refitting and modernizations in December 1942, this time at the Navy Yard, Pearl Harbor. This series of photos was taken on December 12, as the work neared completion. The two 20 mm guns and two splinter shields on the forecastle deck, which had been installed in early 1942, were replaced by new splinter shields, each with two 20 mm gun mounts inside. To the front of the starboard splinter shield is a 20 mm ammunition locker awaiting installation. In the background, significant revisions have been made to the forward superstructure. The original pilothouse has been dismantled and relocated one level below its original level, visible just above the roof of turret number 2. Likewise, the navigating bridge has been lowered to the level where the pilothouse had been, with corresponding changes to the bulwark, and a Mk. 33 secondary-battery director with a fire-control radar antenna has been mounted on the new navigating bridge. That director is trained to port, and the canvas cover has been removed.

Changes visible in this view of the aft starboard side of *Indianapolis* include the presence of a single 20 mm gun in a splinter shield on the roof of turret number 3. The turret enclosures were referred to as gunhouses and were constructed of relatively thin armor, proof mostly against splinters. The two 20 mm guns and splinter shields on the fantail had been replaced by two 40 mm gun mounts with Mk. 51 directors in the small tubs mounted atop the splinter shields, part of which is visible to the far right. (Some sources mistakenly insist that two quadruple 1.1-inch gun mounts were installed on the fantail in late 1942.) A very close inspection of the photo reveals that the right mount has four spent-casing chutes, which indicates a quadruple mount. As will be seen, by May 1943, both 40 mm mounts on the fantail were twin mounts.

In the final photo taken on December 12, 1942, on the starboard side of the forward fire-control station, the upper platform of the foretop, is a 20 mm gun mount. A similar mount was on the port side. Atop the receiver of the gun is a Sperry Mk. 14 computing gunsight. The power unit for the sight is mounted at the bottom of the gun shield. Under the receiver is a canvas bag for collecting spent casings. To the right is the foundation of the forward main-battery director.

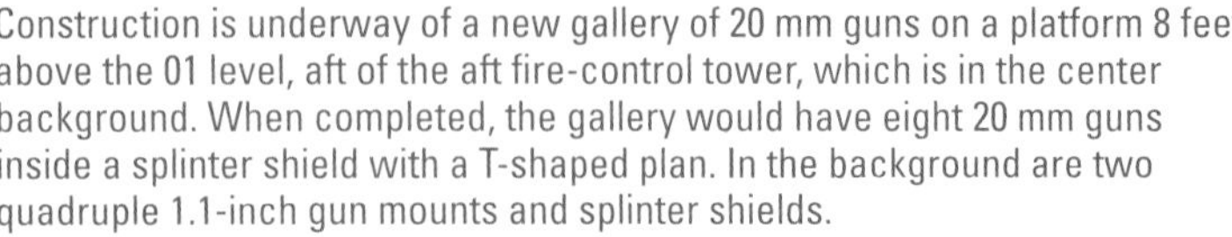
Construction is underway of a new gallery of 20 mm guns on a platform 8 feet above the 01 level, aft of the aft fire-control tower, which is in the center background. When completed, the gallery would have eight 20 mm guns inside a splinter shield with a T-shaped plan. In the background are two quadruple 1.1-inch gun mounts and splinter shields.

During the December 1942 work at Pearl Harbor, two 20 mm gun mounts were installed on each side of the communication platform, or the 01 level, abeam the forward end of the superstructure. The mounts on the port side are shown, and the mounts were arranged similarly on the starboard side. To the upper left is the pilothouse, and to the right is a quadruple 1.1-inch gun mount, with the port catapult to the rear.

On December 14, 1942, *Indianapolis* is running at speed off the coast of Oahu, in a test of the ship's performance following her refitting. The two main-battery directors and the two secondary-battery directors all had been fitted with fire-control radar antennas.

Indianapolis is seen from overhead, slightly to port, as she proceeds at speed off Oahu on December 14, 1942. The new, T-shaped platform with a gallery of eight 20 mm guns is to the front of the mainmast. The two new splinter shields for 20 mm gun mounts are visible on the forecastle deck.

During her yard time at Pearl Harbor in December 1942, as seen in a photo dated December 22, 1942, *Indianapolis*'s Navy Blue camouflage paint was renewed. Casting an angled shadow on the hull below the forward smokestack is a boat boom. Curtiss SOC Seagull scout planes are now aboard. The new platform with a gallery of eight 20 mm guns is easily discerned to the front of the mainmast. *US Navy via A. D. Baker III*

In December 1942, USS *Indianapolis* is steaming off a coastline, probably that of Oahu, around the conclusion of her period of renovations at Pearl Harbor. The new fire-control radar installation on the forward Mk. 33 director was light colored, contrasting with the Navy Blue paint of the ship. *US Navy via A. D. Baker III*

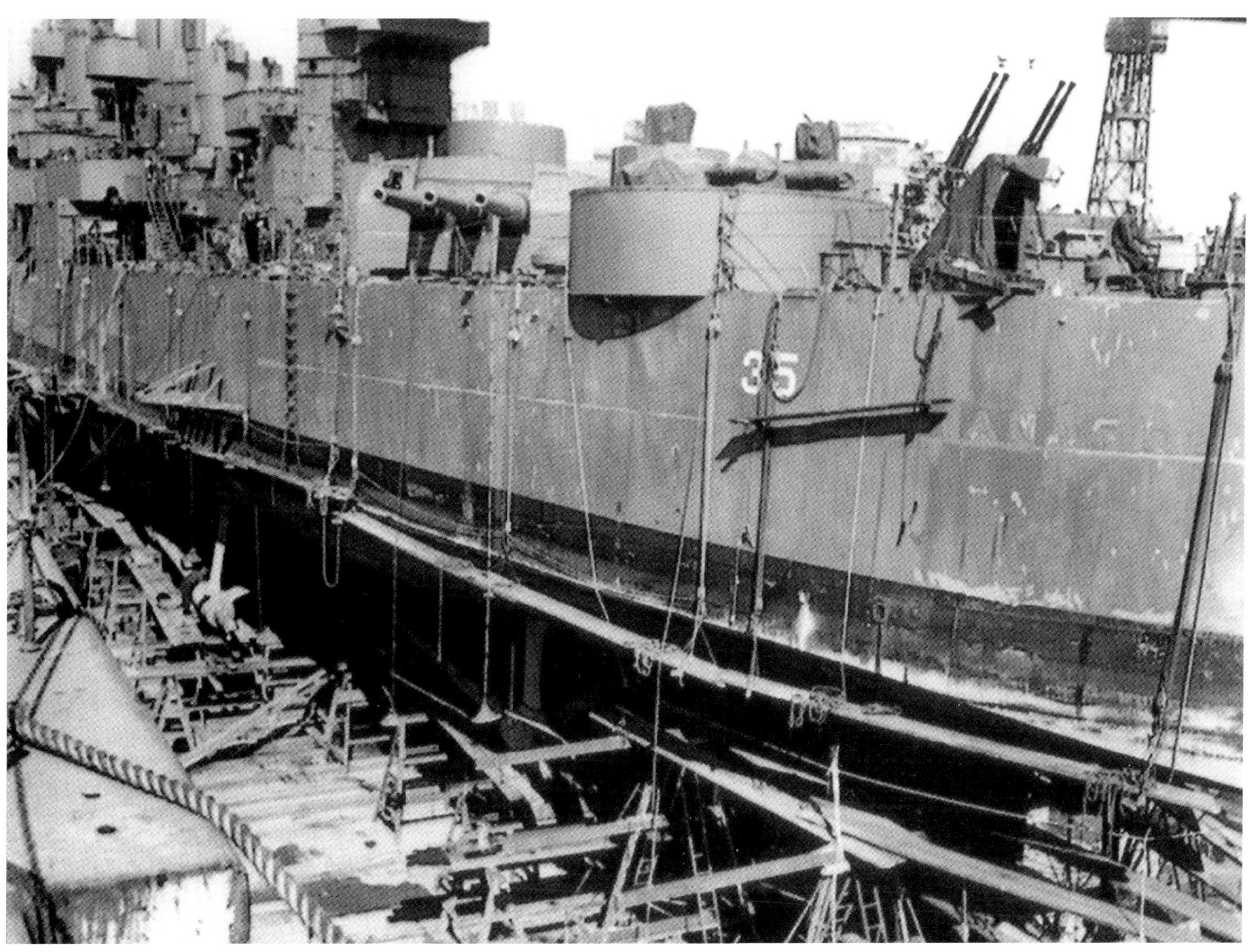

The 40 mm gun mounts, as seen here, were first installed on the fantail in December 1942, and at that time the old aft fire-control tower forward of turret 3, which supported the aft 5-inch-gun director, was still there, as seen in this photo. The May 1943 photos of the ship during refitting at Mare Island show the ship after the tower supporting the aft director was removed and the director was remounted on a pedestal. Two quad 40 mm mounts remain on the fantail. Photos taken toward the end of the May 1943 modernizations show that those quad mounts have been replaced by two twin 40 mm mounts on the fantail. *US Naval Institute / Alfred J. Sedivi Collection*

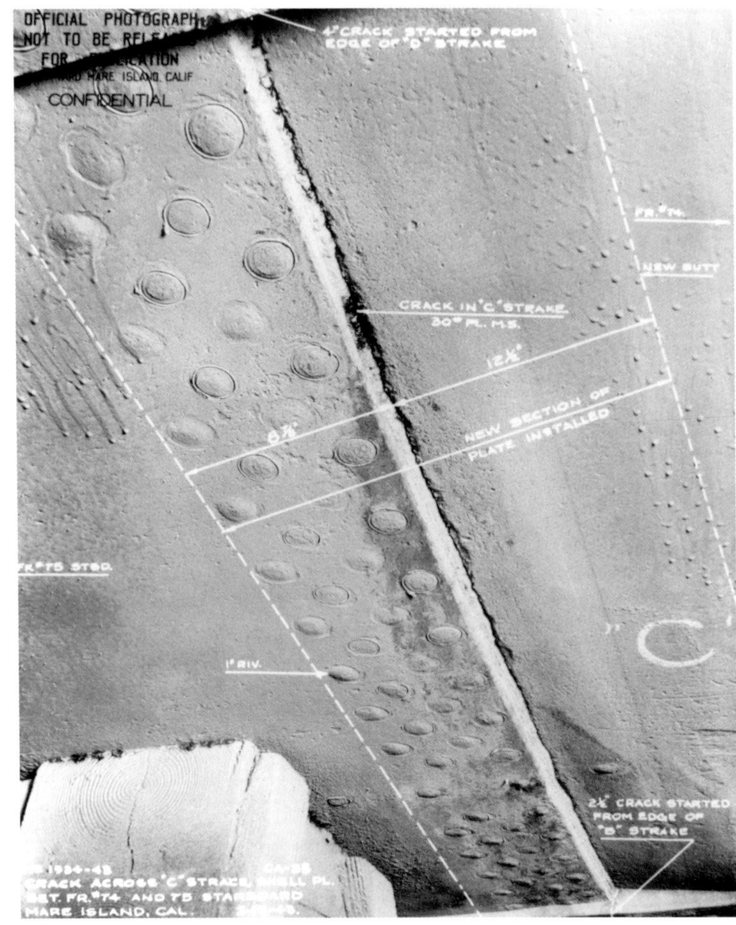

Indianapolis returned to Mare Island Naval Shipyard, in Vallejo, California, for repairs and refitting in early 1943. This photo taken while the ship was in drydock on March 19 shows cracks in the lower part of the shell—the outer skin of the hull—along the "C" strake between frames 74 and 75 on the starboard side. Notations and lines indicate the damage and the location of new plates to be installed to repair the damage. *Mare Island Museum*

This April 7, 1943, photo documents a fracture in the port strut of the foremast (*center*) below the communication platform (*top*). Indicated to the left are several welded repairs to cracks in the communication platform and bulkhead 55 port, below it. *Mare Island Museum*

At Mare Island, a fracture was repaired on the starboard foremast strut (*center*) below the communications platform (*top*). A section of the bulkhead was cut away, to the left, to allow access to the fracture. *Mare Island Museum*

This sequence of photos was taken on May 1, 1943, near the end of *Indianapolis*'s period of repairs and modernization at Mare Island from March to May of that year. Areas of interest in the photos were outlined. One change since the overhaul at Pearl Harbor in December 1942 was that cutouts had been made toward the bottoms of the splinter shields for the 20 mm guns on the forecastle. Drastic changes had been made to the foretop above the tripod foremast, in the interest of reducing obstructions to antiaircraft spotting and firing. The fire-control platform has been removed, and a much-smaller platform with a bulwark and small wings has been installed at that level. The Mk. 27 main-battery director and Mk. 3 fire-control radar antenna remain at the top of the foretop.

As seen from off the port beam amidships, the mainmast was removed from the rear of the superstructure, and a new tripod mainmast was installed to the front of the aft smokestack on *Indianapolis* at Mare Island in early spring 1943. The mainmast now supported an SK air-search radar antenna, partly visible above the platform to the upper left.

In a view of the starboard side of *Indianapolis* from the forward smokestack (*right*) aft, the lower part of the new tripod mainmast is above the new deckhouse, which housed the secondary steering station, the smokestack. To the lower right are floater nets, which were being introduced to the ship. These nets would float free of the ship in the event it sank, providing crewmen with the means of remaining afloat until rescuers could arrive. These nets would figure prominently in the story of *Indianapolis* when it was sunk. New port and starboard hangar doors have been installed. These doors were of folding, rather than the original rollup, design. The port door is open, while the starboard one is closed; on the inboard side of that door is a small door for personnel to enter or exit without opening the entire door.

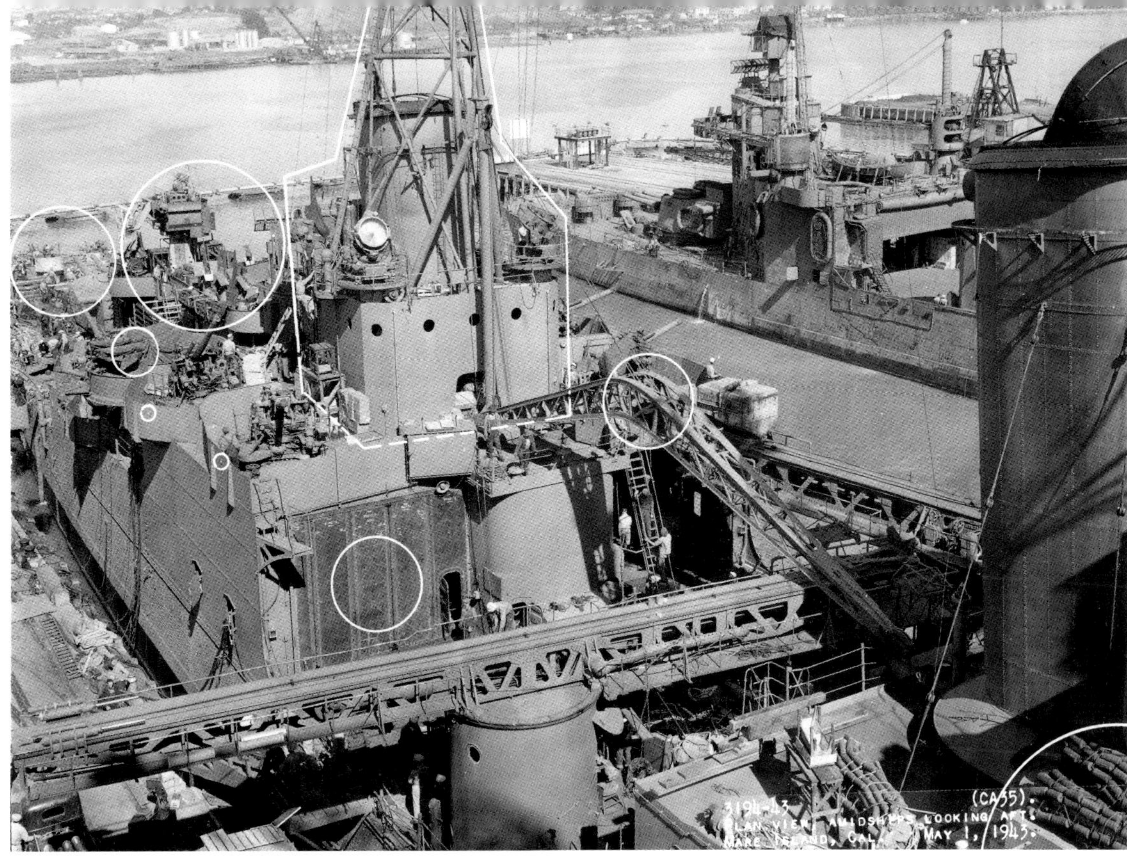

Atop the aft superstructure toward the left, which contained an ordnance workshop and crew facilities, the aft Mk. 33 secondary-battery director now has been installed on a pedestal; it is equipped with a Mk. 4 fire-control radar antenna. Here, the director is trained to starboard. Floater nets are stowed along the bulwark below the director. Farther forward and aft of the aft smokestack is the aft main-battery director with fire-control radar antenna.

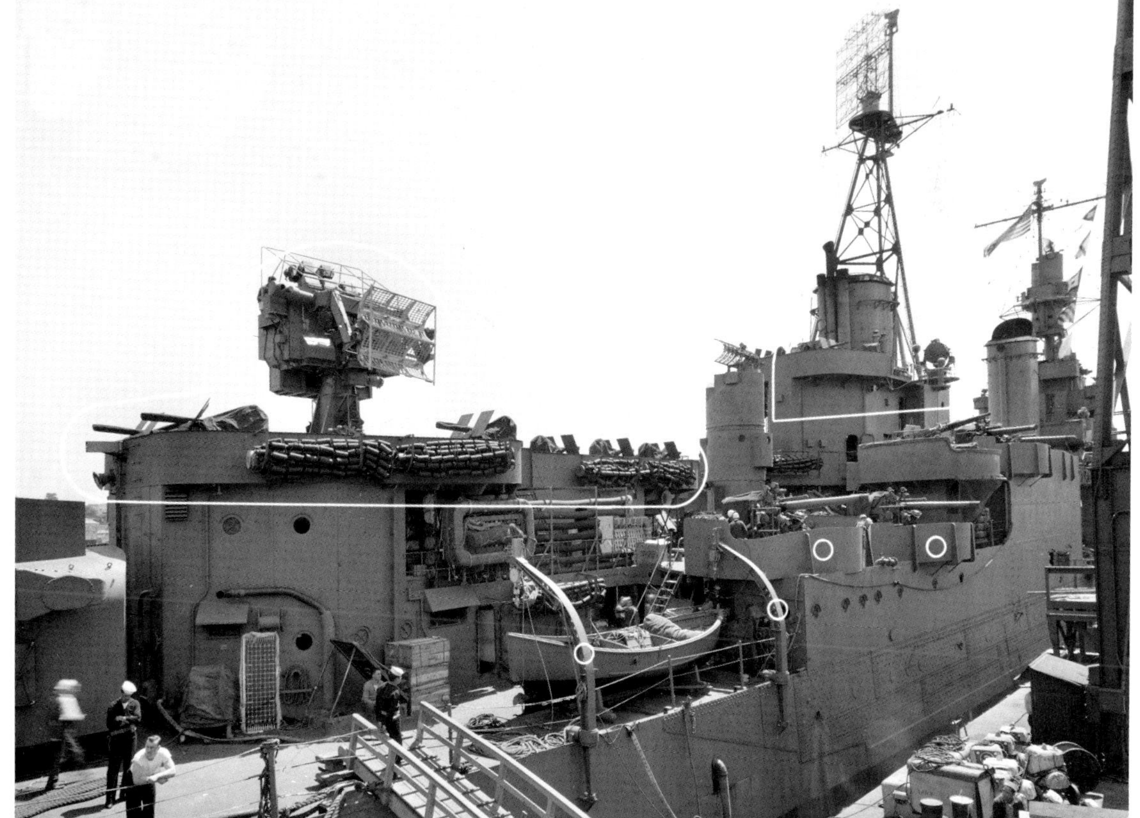

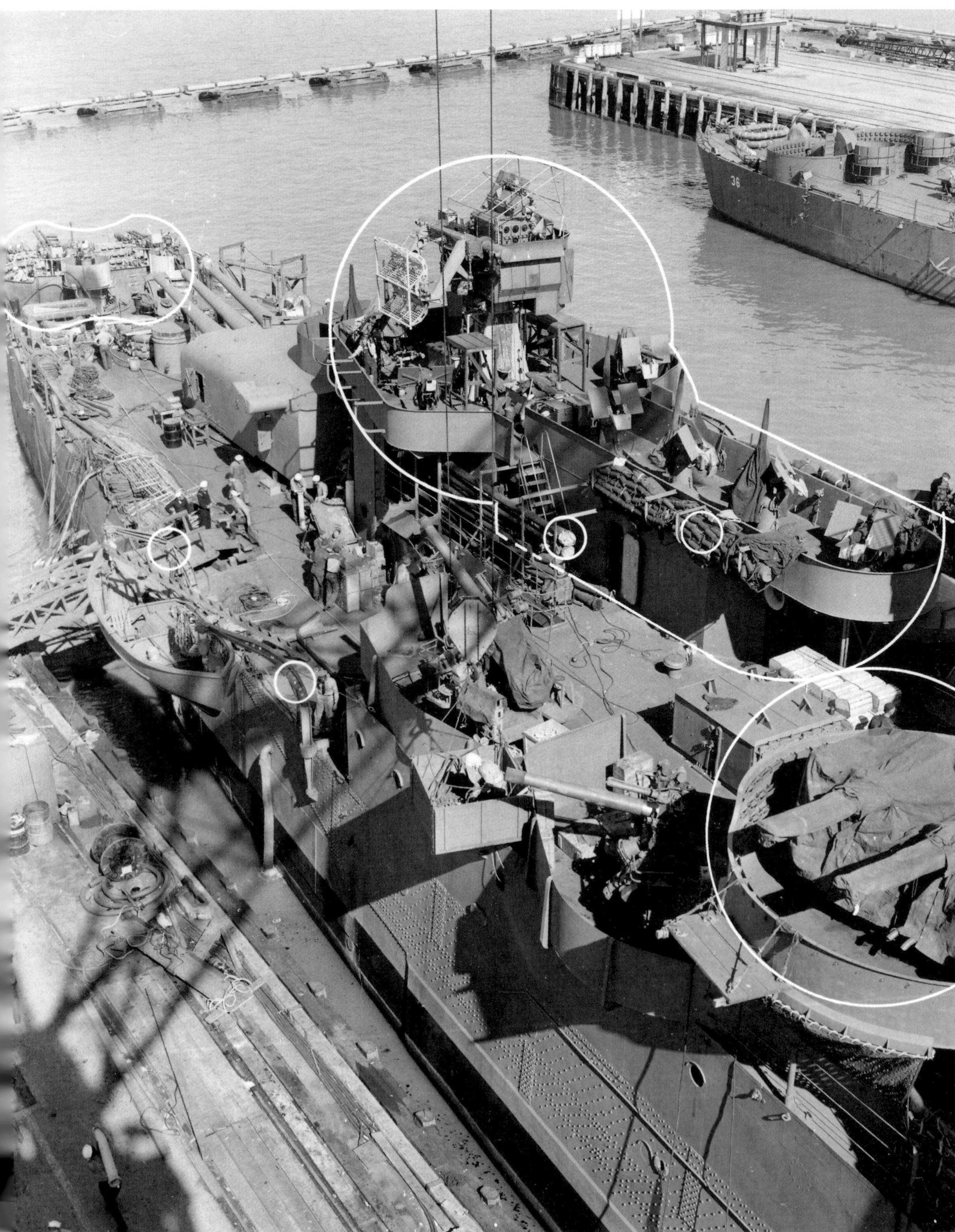

The aft superstructure, the T-shaped 20 mm gun platform, turret number 3, and the fantail are viewed from the starboard side at Mare Island on May 1, 1943. In the foreground is a newly installed quadruple 40 mm gun mount with a cover over the entire mount. Forward of the gangplank is a 26-foot motor whaleboat on davits. On the fantail are two twin 40 mm gun mounts.

On May 2, 1943, the day after the preceding sequence of photos was taken, the newly modernized *Indianapolis* was photographed off Mare Island, California. Surface-search radar antennas were on the tops of the foremast and the mainmast, and the SK air-search radar antenna is faintly visible below the SG surface-search radar antenna on the mainmast. The two chains to the front of the bow were part of the equipment for the paravanes: devices carried on warships to cut the moorings of submerged mines.

The port profile of *Indianapolis* is beautifully portrayed after her spring 1943 modernizations. The two main-battery directors are perched on their comparatively narrow pedestals. The extensively redesigned forward superstructure and fire-control tower may be compared with pre-1943 photos of the same structure.

USS *Indianapolis* is observed from off the port stern on May 2, 1943. The two depth-charge racks on the fantail had been eliminated, but the smoke generators were still in position there. *US Navy via A. D. Baker III*

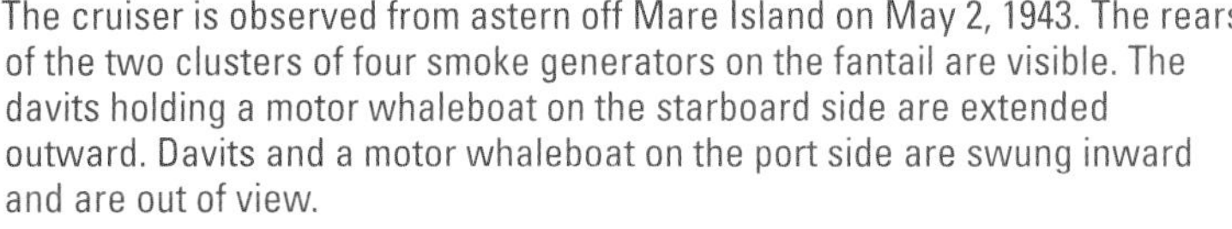

The cruiser is observed from astern off Mare Island on May 2, 1943. The rears of the two clusters of four smoke generators on the fantail are visible. The davits holding a motor whaleboat on the starboard side are extended outward. Davits and a motor whaleboat on the port side are swung inward and are out of view.

USS *Indianapolis* exhibits a slight list to port in this May 2, 1943, photo and the preceding one. The rounded platforms extending from the communication platform in the background, which originally held quadruple 1.1-inch gun mounts, now were equipped with quad 40 mm gun mounts. These mounts have dark-colored covers over them. At this time, the forward Mk. 33 director for the 5-inch guns had a cowling on the front, which covered the better part of the rangefinder except for its outer ends. At the top of the front of the cowling was a venturi windscreen, to protect the crew of the rangefinder from winds. The aft Mk. 33 lacked this cowling.

USS *Indianapolis* returned to the Aleutians in the summer of 1943. In a photo taken from USS *Salt Lake City* (CA-25) on August 2, 1943, *Indianapolis* is in the foreground, part of a force of warships bombarding Japanese positions on Kiska. Ironically, the last of the Japanese occupiers of that island had evacuated it on July 28. The raised, boxy shape of the aft Mk. 33 director is prominent to the rear of the aft smokestack.

The bombardment of Kiska continued for two weeks after the initial bombardment of August 2, 1943. All that was accomplished was the destruction of abandoned Japanese facilities and vessels at the port. Here, *Indianapolis*'s three turrets are trained to starboard during the shelling of Kiska on August 8, 1943.

Indianapolis is viewed from a scout plane off her starboard stern during the naval bombardment of Kiska on August 10, 1943. The story behind the light-colored areas on the decks is unclear. The area on the aft part of the main deck, including below turret 3, appears to be painted a light color, or possibly is bare wood, while other light-colored areas farther forward seem to be light-colored fabric. Some of the light-colored areas are visible, only very faintly, in the preceding photo. In August 1943, *Indianapolis* was assigned four Curtiss SOC-1s from VCS-4, and one of them is on each catapult.

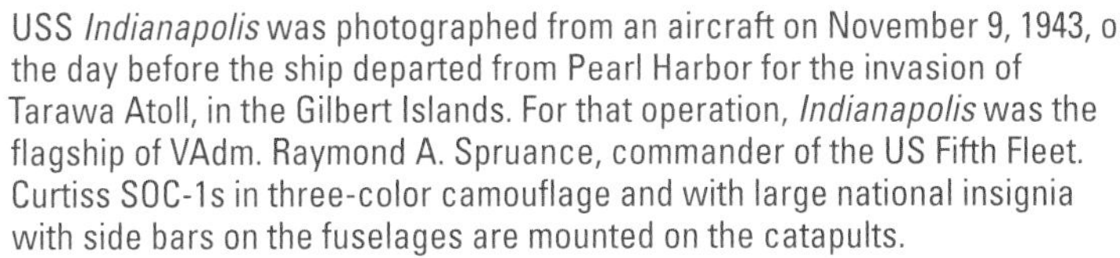

USS *Indianapolis* was photographed from an aircraft on November 9, 1943, on the day before the ship departed from Pearl Harbor for the invasion of Tarawa Atoll, in the Gilbert Islands. For that operation, *Indianapolis* was the flagship of VAdm. Raymond A. Spruance, commander of the US Fifth Fleet. Curtiss SOC-1s in three-color camouflage and with large national insignia with side bars on the fuselages are mounted on the catapults.

Indianapolis again served as the flagship of VAdm. Raymond Spruance for Operation Flintlock: the campaign to defeat the Japanese on Kwajalein and Majuro, in the Marshall Islands, in late January and early February 1944. In a photo taken next to a twin 5-inch/38-caliber gun mount on the carrier USS *Intrepid* (CV-11), *Indianapolis* is underway at Majuro Atoll, in the eastern Marshall Islands, on February 7, 1944, a week after US forces captured that atoll. Sometime between when the photos of the ship were taken in November 1943 and the time this one was taken, a hood was installed on the forward part of the top of the aft smokestack, similar to the one that had existed on the forward stack for some time.

The following series of images are stills from a color film taken of *Indianapolis* underway in the Pacific in February 1944. Here, the starboard side is in view from the bow to the foretop. Prominent above the navigating bridge is the pedestal-mounted forward Mk. 33 director.

In a motion-picture frame similar to the preceding one, the aircraft crane is in its raised position to the front of the mainmast.

The starboard amidships area is depicted, showing the recently installed hood on the top of the aft smokestack.

To the left of center in this frame is the aft primary-battery director, with fire-control radar antenna on top. To the left of that feature is the forward part of the gallery of eight 20 mm gun mounts; the gun shields of the forward four mounts are visible above the splinter shield.

The aft part of *Indianapolis* is shown in this frame, with the aft main-battery director to the right, the 20 mm gun gallery and the aft Mk. 33 director to the right of center, and turret 3 and the stern to the left.

More of the midships area of the starboard side is in view, including the aircraft crane to the far left.

The forward half of *Indianapolis* is in view, with an unidentified warship in the background.

In another still from color motion-picture footage, taken in March 1944, crewmen and officers of *Indianapolis* are gathered on the forecastle. Below and to the front of the three 8-inch guns are 20 mm gun galleries.

Officers are on the navigating bridge of *Indianapolis*. Jutting from the top of the bulwark are venturi windscreens, which directed the wind upward, sparing the personnel on the bridge from the full effect of a strong wind. Directly above the navigating bridge is the forward Mk. 33 secondary-battery director, the crew of which controlled the firing of the ship's 5-inch/25-caliber guns.

A final still from wartime color movie footage shows turret 3, the navigating bridge, the forward Mk. 33 director and its white- or light-gray-colored Mk. 4 fire-control radar antenna, and, at the top, the forward primary-battery director, directly below which is the forward fire-control station.

An undated photograph depicts the mainmast of *Indianapolis* as it generally appeared between the time it was installed at Mare Island in April 1943 and November 1944, when, again at Mare Island, a new platform was installed just below the big platform at the top of the tripod, two small platforms were mounted below the SG radar, and yet another upper mast was added. The SK air-search "bed spring" radar antenna is atop the platform in this photo, and the SG surface-search radar is atop the upper mast. *US Naval Institute / Alfred J. Sedivi Collection*

Between operations in the Pacific, *Indianapolis* was used to transport personnel to California, arriving on April 21, 1944. While at San Francisco, the ship received a new camouflage scheme, Measure 32/7D. This consisted of splinter patterns on the vertical surfaces above the waterline of Light Gray (5-L), Ocean Gray (5-O), and Black (BK), and splinter patterns on horizontal surfaces of Deck Blue (20-B) and Ocean Gray. The cruiser was photographed in that new camouflage off the US Naval Dry Docks at Hunters Point, San Francisco, on May 1, 1944. *US Navy via A. D. Baker III*

Indianapolis is viewed broadside from the port beam on May 1, 1944. The idea of the Measure 32 camouflage was to confound enemy attempts to discern, identify, and plot the bearing of the ship. Two Curtiss SOC-1 scout planes are mounted on the port catapult. *US Navy via A. D. Baker III*

Off Hunters Point on May 1, 1944, *Indianapolis* is viewed from off her port stern. The Mk. 4 radar antenna of the Mk. 33 director (*above and forward of turret 3*) has been swung down in front of the director, which is trained to the rear. *US Navy via A. D. Baker III*

A tugboat is steaming off the starboard beam of *Indianapolis* in San Francisco Bay on May 1, 1944. Some of the demarcations between the Deck Blue and the lighter Ocean Gray on the decks and horizontal surfaces are visible. *US Navy via A. D. Baker III*

Indianapolis is viewed from an altitude of 400 feet while underway in San Francisco Bay on May 1, 1944. The new Measure 32/7D camouflage on the starboard side is seen with the cruiser backlit.

In a frontal view of *Indianapolis* docked at San Francisco, California, on May 1, 1944, arrows and numbers refer to the various colors of paint applied as part of the 7D scheme. The cowling on the front of the forward Mk. 33 director, present when the director was installed at Mare Island in the spring of 1943, has since been removed. The director is trained partially to starboard, and the entirety of the rangefinder on the front of the director is visible with the cowling removed. Right below the director, an awning has been erected over the navigating bridge. *US Navy via A. D. Baker III*

With the Mk. 33 director trained forward, more details are visible of the central part of its rangefinder. The rangefinder was designed to pivot laterally, in order to remain level as the ship rolled. The life raft lashed to the side of the gunhouse of turret 1 contains survival supplies and equipment.

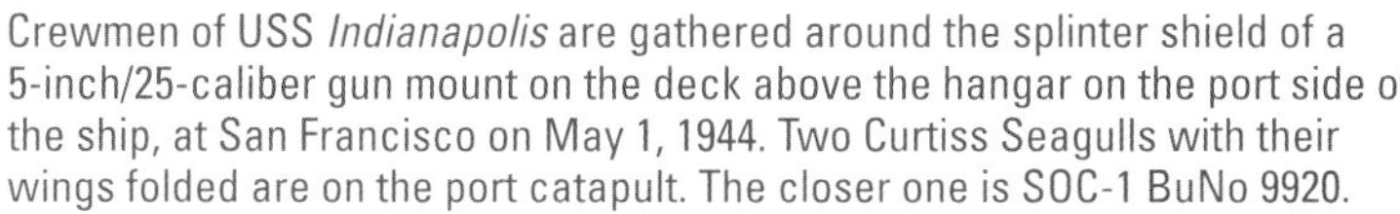
Crewmen of USS *Indianapolis* are gathered around the splinter shield of a 5-inch/25-caliber gun mount on the deck above the hangar on the port side of the ship, at San Francisco on May 1, 1944. Two Curtiss Seagulls with their wings folded are on the port catapult. The closer one is SOC-1 BuNo 9920.

A view along the port side of *Indianapolis* includes a rare near view of the 8-inch guns elevated on turret number 3. Piled on the roof of that turret are floater nets. Aft of the turret are two ventilators and a winch. The aft Mk. 33 director is on a pedestal at the rear of the 20 mm gun gallery forward of turret 3. Unlike the forward Mk. 33 director, which had the fire-control radar mounted above it, the aft Mk. 33 director's radar antenna was on arms mounted on the rangefinder on the front of the director. A canvas top is fitted over bows on the top of the director, with a flap on the center of the cover opened.

After her refitting was completed at San Francisco, *Indianapolis* participated in the Marianas Campaign. A photographer aboard USS *Birmingham* (CL-62) took this view of *Indianapolis* during one of the invasions in that campaign, in June 1944: presumably Saipan. Landing craft are faintly visible in the background, streaming toward the beachhead. *Indianapolis* was the flagship of Adm. Raymond Spruance during this battle.

During D-day at Saipan, on June 15, 1944, USS *Indianapolis* stood offshore, shelling Japanese positions. During the battle, a Japanese 120 mm shell struck *Indianapolis*, but it proved to be a dud. Here, two shells from Japanese shore batteries have just struck the water off the cruiser's port beam.

Indianapolis's new Measure 32/7D camouflage scheme is particularly striking in this photo of the ship's 8-inch guns in turrets 1 and 2 shelling Japanese forces on Saipan on June 15, 1944. *US Navy via A. D. Baker III*

In a photo taken from USS *Birmingham,* whose aft turret and fantail are in the foreground, *Indianapolis*'s 8-inch/55-caliber guns have just unleashed a salvo on Japanese strongpoints on Saipan, on June 15, 1944. Between the two ships, LVTs are proceeding toward shore.

USS *Indianapolis* is steaming off Saipan on June 15, 1944, as photographed from USS *Birmingham. Indianapolis's* catapults are empty, the scout planes having taken off to perform artillery spotting for the cruiser's gunners.

Adm. Ernest J. King, commander in chief of the US Fleet as well as chief of naval operations (*center*), is visiting USS *Indianapolis* on July 18, 1944, between the conclusion of the Battle of Saipan and the beginning of the invasions of Guam and Tinian. Posing with him are Adm. Chester W. Nimitz, commander in chief of the Pacific Fleet and Pacific Ocean Areas (*left*), and Adm. Raymond A. Spruance, commander of the Fifth Fleet (*right*). Following the sinking of *Indianapolis* a year later, Adm. King would press for the court-martial of the commanding officer of the cruiser at that time, Capt. Charles B. McVay III.

The following color motion-picture stills depict USS *Indianapolis* during a lull in the fighting in the Marianas in July 1944. The Measure 32/7D paint, which was applied to the cruiser in April, already is showing much wear on the bow and above the waterline.

The dissimilar camouflage patterns on the starboard and port sides of the hull are evident in this image taken off the bow.

The wings of the ship's Curtiss SOC Seagull scout planes are visible on both sides of *Indianapolis*, amidships. A small awning has been rigged over the forecastle.

The final color film still from July 1944 shows *Indianapolis* off her starboard bow, at anchor. The aircraft crane is in its raised position, forward of the aft smokestack.

Operating alongside USS *Birmingham*, from which this photo was taken, USS *Indianapolis* participated in the landings on Tinian, in the Mariana Islands, on July 24, 1944, providing fire support for the invasion force.

On August 19, 1944, the date that organized Japanese resistance ended on Guam, USS *Indianapolis* is anchored in Apra Harbor, Guam, as photographed from the Orote Peninsula. A close inspection of the photo shows that *Indianapolis* still has the Mk. 27 directors on the foretop and in the aft positions. This would change sometime during the following month.

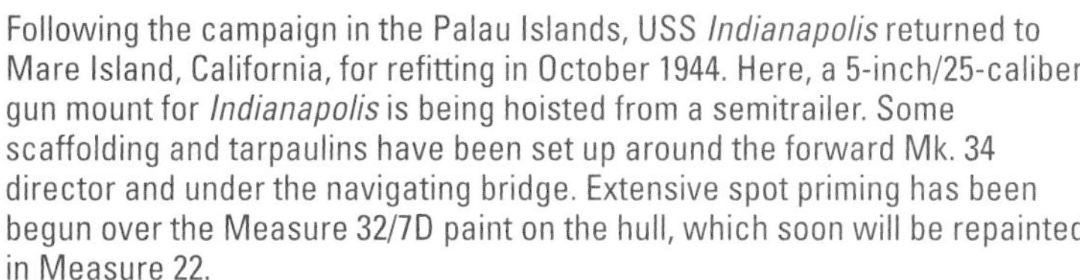

Following the campaign in the Palau Islands, USS *Indianapolis* returned to Mare Island, California, for refitting in October 1944. Here, a 5-inch/25-caliber gun mount for *Indianapolis* is being hoisted from a semitrailer. Some scaffolding and tarpaulins have been set up around the forward Mk. 34 director and under the navigating bridge. Extensive spot priming has been begun over the Measure 32/7D paint on the hull, which soon will be repainted in Measure 22.

A 5-inch/25-caliber gun mount is being hoisted onto *Indianapolis.* Painted on the mount is "#3," which probably is a reference to the mount's number on the ship. On the left rear of the mount are fuse setters. Mount number 3 was the second one from the front on the starboard side of the deck over the hangar.

This and the next three photos were taken during inclining experiments on the *Indianapolis* toward the end of her refitting at Mare Island, on November 26, 1944. These experiments, conducted after any major refitting, established the center of gravity and other data essential for the stability and safe operation of the ship. In the foreground is quadruple 40 mm gun mount number 2, with a pedestal and shield for a 20 mm gun just forward of it. On the bulwark of the navigating bridge is a scoreboard, with symbols for destroyed Japanese ships, aircraft, and other targets marked on it.

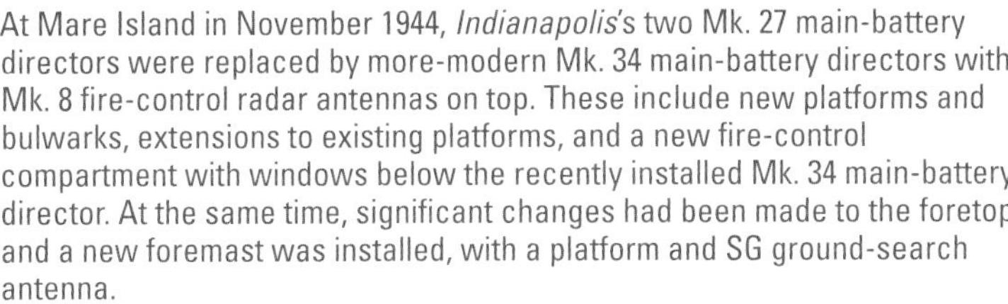

At Mare Island in November 1944, *Indianapolis*'s two Mk. 27 main-battery directors were replaced by more-modern Mk. 34 main-battery directors with Mk. 8 fire-control radar antennas on top. These include new platforms and bulwarks, extensions to existing platforms, and a new fire-control compartment with windows below the recently installed Mk. 34 main-battery director. At the same time, significant changes had been made to the foretop, and a new foremast was installed, with a platform and SG ground-search antenna.

Indianapolis is viewed from next to the port catapult to the rear, showing the mainmast with the SK air-search radar antenna toward the top. An SG surface-search radar antenna is at the very top of the mainmast. Next to the catapult is the lowered aircraft crane. To the sides of the aft smokestack are two 36-inch searchlights. To the rear are the aft Mk. 34 director and Mk. 8 radar, and the aft Mk. 33 secondary-battery director, which now had an enclosed top and a new fire-control radar on the front: the Mk. 25, with a dish-type antenna.

The aft Mk. 34 director (*upper center*) and aft Mk. 33 director (*toward the right*) are seen from a different perspective, with the Mk. 25 antenna on the Mk. 33 director, which is trained to starboard, more visible. In the foreground are a 5-inch/25-caliber gun mount and a quadruple 40 mm gun mount. These photos show that by November 26, 1944, the Measure 32/7D camouflage scheme had been painted over with Measure 22, with Navy Blue (5-N) on the hull from the waterline up to the main deck, Haze Gray (5-H) on vertical surfaces from the main deck up, and Weatherdeck Blue (20-B) on decks and horizontal surfaces.

Twelve days after the inclining experiments, a photographer took this view of the forward part of *Indianapolis* from the port side. Numerous 8-inch shells are lined up on the communication platform to the port side of turret 2. A paravane, for cutting mooring lines of submerged mines, is stored on the corner of the superstructure to the side of turret 2. Numerous bins made of expanded-steel mesh and steel frames had been installed on the ship to hold floater nets; one of these is visible to the lower right. At the top right is the redesigned fire-control station.

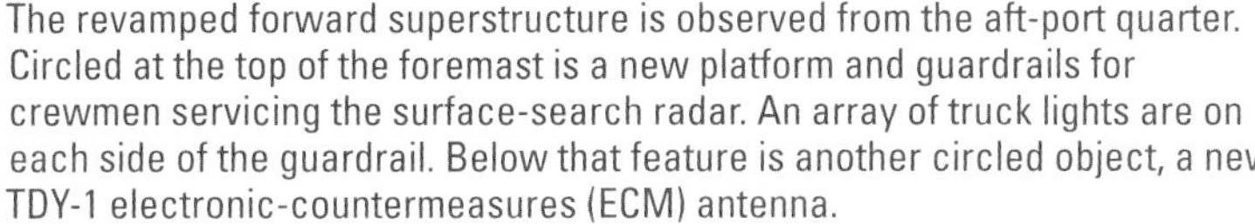

The revamped forward superstructure is observed from the aft-port quarter. Circled at the top of the foremast is a new platform and guardrails for crewmen servicing the surface-search radar. An array of truck lights are on each side of the guardrail. Below that feature is another circled object, a new TDY-1 electronic-countermeasures (ECM) antenna.

Several new features are circled on this photo taken at Mare Island on December 7, 1944. To the left is a whip antenna on the side of the smokestack. Faintly visible at the top of the mainmast is a new extension to the mast, on the top of which is a DQ direction-finder antenna. Below the base of that extension is the SG surface-search radar, on a new, oblong platform, just below which is a new work platform with guardrail. Circled on the tripod part of the mainmast is another new platform with guardrails.

During the refitting of *Indianapolis* at Mare Island in late 1944, the two twin 40 mm gun mounts on the fantail were replaced by two quadruple 40 mm gun mounts. To make room for the new mounts, the splinter shield was extended to the front, with the two Mk. 51 director tubs now straddling it. The splinter shield also was extended on the sides, to overhang the hull. The new Mk. 25 fire-control radar antenna is on the front of the Mk. 33 director. The figure-8 outline to the left of the Mk. 25 antenna delineates the tower recently installed to support the aft Mk. 34 main-battery director. At the base of the tower is a new platform and bulwark, on each side of which is a Mk. 51 director for controlling the 40 mm gun batteries.

Indianapolis is underway off Mare Island, California, on December 9, 1944, exhibiting new and recent features such as the redesigned foretop and masts, and the Measure 22 camouflage scheme. *US Navy via A. D. Baker III*

USS *Indianapolis* presents her starboard profile off Mare Island on December 9, 1944, presenting a clear picture of the new shape of the foretop and the masts.

The cruiser is viewed just above the water, 135 degrees off its fore-and-aft centerline, off Mare Island on December 9, 1944. The Mk. 8 fire-control radar antennas are clearly visible above the Mk. 34 primary-battery directors. *US Navy via A. D. Baker III*

A broadside view taken off the port side of *Indianapolis* off Mare Island on December 9, 1944, again shows the new Measure 22 camouflage. The cruiser's number, 35, is painted on the bow in white, 2 feet high. *US Navy via A. D. Baker III*

Indianapolis is observed from dead astern on December 9, 1944. The black band visible above the waterline is the boot topping: a treatment applied above and below the waterline to disguise the oil, grease, and other contaminants that tend to float on the surface of harbors and collect on hulls. *US Navy via A. D. Baker III*

A comparison of the earlier frontal view of *Indianapolis* with this December 9, 1944, view emphasizes the significant visual changes to the ship during the twelve years since its commissioning. The yardarm of the foremast was now equipped with a BK IFF (identification, friend or foe) "ski pole" antenna on each side, as well as an anemometer and wind vane near the center of the starboard side, and a TBS VHF radio antenna toward the center of the port side. *US Navy via A. D. Baker III*

As photographed from an aircraft, *Indianapolis* is underway on December 14, 1944. Exactly one month later, the cruiser would meet up with Task Force 58, which would commence carrier airstrikes against the Japanese home islands. *US Navy via A. D. Baker III*

The starboard side of USS *Indianapolis* is viewed from an aircraft on December 14, 1944. The two masts and the radar and antenna arrays, which often are difficult to discern, are more visible here against the backdrop of the ocean. Dark-colored fairings now are installed over the Mk. 8 fire-control radar antennas above the Mk. 34 primary-battery directors. *US Navy via A. D. Baker III*

An injured sailor is being moved on a stretcher aboard *Indianapolis* during February 1945. The scene is at the ladder leading down from the port side of the gallery of eight 20 mm antiaircraft guns to the rear of the aft main-battery director. Several of those gun mounts are in view. In the left foreground are floater nets in their storage bins. In this immediate area, a Japanese kamikaze plane would crash into the ship on March 31, 1945.

Adm. Raymond Spruance, *left*, commander of the US Fifth Fleet, and FAdm. Chester Nimitz, commander in chief of the Pacific Fleet (CINCPAC), pause for their portrait while aboard USS *Indianapolis* at Guam in February 1945.

Specifications	
Class and type	Portland-class cruiser
Displacement	9,950 long tons (standard)
Length	610 ft., 3 in. overall
	584 ft. waterline
Beam	66 ft., 1 in.
Draft	17 ft., 4 in. (mean)
	24 ft. (max.)
Engineering	8 × White-Forster boilers
	4 × Parsons reduction steam turbines. 107,000 shp
	4 × screws
Speed	32.7 knots
Complement	46 officers, 906 enlisted (as designed)
	100 officers, 1,282 enlisted (wartime)
Armament, as built	9 × 8-inch/55-caliber guns in three triple turrets
	8 × 5-inch/25-caliber antiaircraft guns
	2 × 3-pounder saluting guns
	8 × .50-caliber machine guns
Aircraft carried	4 × floatplanes
Aviation facilities	2 × amidships catapults
Armament 1945	9 × 8-inch/55-caliber guns in three triple turrets
	8 × 5 inch/25-caliber antiaircraft guns
	2 × 3-pounder saluting guns
	6 × quad 40 mm Bofors antiaircraft guns
	16 × single 20 mm Oerlikon antiaircraft cannons
Aircraft carried	3 × floatplanes
Aviation facilities	1 × amidships catapults (starboard catapult removed in 1945)
Armor	Belt: 3¼–5 in.
	Deck: 2½ in.
	Barbettes: 1½ in.
	Turrets: 1½–2½ in.
	Conning tower: 1¼ in.

On or around February 16, 1945, at a time when *Indianapolis* was operating with a carrier task force conducting airstrikes on Tokyo, a photographer captured this view of the ship from the searchlight platform on the forward-port quarter of the aft smokestack, facing forward. Below are the port catapult, the aircraft crane, and the well deck. Farther forward are the forward smokestack, the mainmast and superstructure, and the 8-inch/55-caliber guns of turrets 1 and 2, trained to port. *US Naval Institute / Alfred J. Sedivi Collection*

CHAPTER 3

Kamikaze!

On March 31, 1945, while operating 11.5 miles off Zampa Misaki, Okinawa, *Indianapolis* was attacked by a Japanese Nakajima Ki-43 Oscar kamikaze plane. Diving at a steep angle, the Oscar crashed into the port side of the main deck between frames 112 and 113. A bomb slung under the plane broke free upon impact and crashed through the decks and the shell of the hull below, exploding just feet below the hull. The damage was serious, but the crew controlled flooding and the ship was able to proceed under her own power. After the kamikaze attack off Okinawa, *Indianapolis* limped to the harbor at Kerama Retto, some 20 miles southwest of Okinawa, for temporary repairs. She was photographed in that harbor from USS *New Mexico* (BB-40) on April 2, 1945. Despite the severe damage the cruiser had suffered, her antiaircraft batteries fired at Japanese aircraft on that date.

While *Indianapolis*'s crew had sustained some casualties, as noted, up to this point, the ship had been largely lucky. That began to change at 0708 on March 31, 1945. A lookout spotted a Nakajima Ki-43 Hayabusa, Allied code name "Oscar," emerging from the clouds in a 65-degree dive toward *Indianapolis*. Eight of the cruiser's 20 mm guns roared into life, firing 392 rounds at the plunging fighter, but before heavier guns could be brought to bear, the Oscar struck *Indianapolis*. Her gunners had damaged the fighter, or its pilot, such that the aircraft missed its apparent intended target, the bridge, its left wingtip instead hitting the floater net rack on the splinter shield of the 20 mm gun platform. This jarring is probably what caused the bomb to release, penetrating the main deck aft near the side of the ship at frame 113, while the aircraft itself toppled into the sea. The bomb destroyed the crew's mess hall, the berthing compartment below, and the fuel tanks still lower before crashing through the bottom of the ship and exploding in the water beneath *Indianapolis*. The blast beneath the ship tore two holes in the ship bottom, with the resulting flooding of compartments and death of nine men. The damage report states, "The ship soon reached its maximum draft and list, and inspection revealed the water-tight boundaries of the damaged areas holding. With the flooding controlled it was decided there was no immediate danger[,] and the ship proceeded to Kerama Retto[,] where emergency repairs were made by USS *Clamp* (ARS33)." The nine dead men were buried at sea, one on March 31, six on April 1, and two on April 2.

Damage assessment revealed that in addition to the damage to the hull, the ship's evaporators were inoperative, the laundry was flooded, several tanks were burst, and the forward strut of the number 4 propeller shaft was torn away, ripping a 2-by-5-foot hole in the hull, which added to the flooding. The shock damage knocked one of *Indianapolis*'s aircraft off its catapult and onto another aircraft stowed on the quarterdeck, damaging both. The port aircraft was knocked askew of its catapult, damaging both.

Personnel from *Clamp*, along with the ship's company, made temporary repairs. Divers placed soft patches over the holes in the hull, and concrete was poured in the interior.

On April 3, Adm. Spruance, still aboard, presented the Purple Heart to sixteen men wounded in the kamikaze attack. On April 5, Spruance transferred his flag to USS *New Mexico* (BB-40)

Indianapolis got underway on April 7, using engines 1 and 2 only, since shaft 3 was unusable due to battle damage and the number 4 propeller had been lost during salvage efforts. Her destination was Apra Harbor, Guam.

At Guam the soft patches were removed and the concrete was chipped out, in order to attempt a more permanent repair. That was found to be impractical, and the soft patches were replaced and new concrete was poured. Additional repairs were made, and the ship got underway on April 15. That same day, at 1310, the ship's company held quarters followed by a five-minute silent and prayer period recognizing the death of president and frequent *Indianapolis* passenger Franklin D. Roosevelt. She arrived off Eniwetok on April 18, where her escorts refueled, before sailing on toward Pearl Harbor, entering the big navy base on April 24.

The initial impact of the Oscar occurred when the left wing plowed into this floater-net bin on the port side of the gallery of eight 20 mm guns. To the left is the aft Mk. 34 director.

The Oscar's engine and the bomb that came loose from the plane (estimated to be a 500-pound bomb) created this large hole in the port side of the main deck, just forward of frame 114.

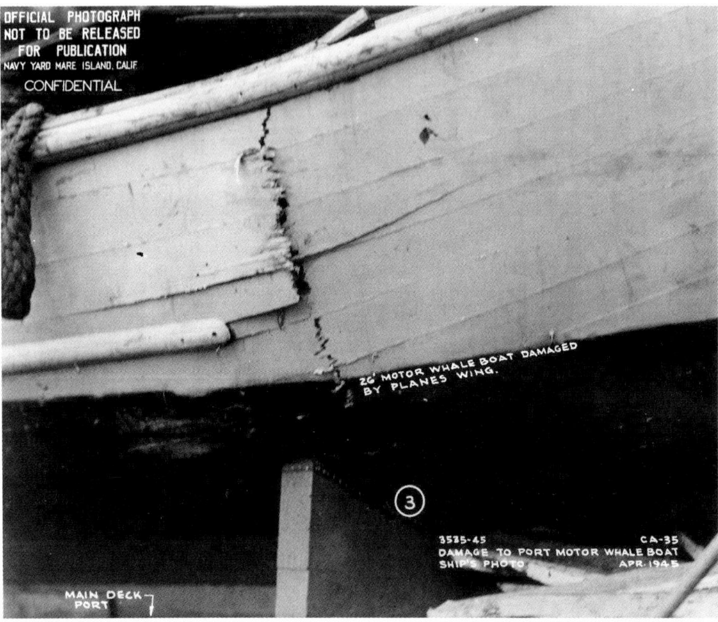

After sawing into the floater-net bin, the Oscar's left wing struck the port 26-foot motor whaleboat, leaving a vertical crack on the side.

The entry hole on the main deck is seen facing aft. The deck armor here was 25-pound high-tensile steel. The kamikaze attack resulted in the deaths of nine crewmen and the wounding of twenty-six.

Rather than being repaired there, on April 26 she steamed without escort toward San Francisco. She reached San Francisco on May, and following an agricultural and customs inspection at berth 7, San Francisco Bay, she steamed to Mare Island Navy Yard and began unloading ammunition. On May 3 she was tied up at Pier 22, and repair work had begun. On May 6 she was moved into drydock, where she would remain, undergoing repair until June 23.

Following testing and recalibration, on July 12, Capt. McVay received orders that he and *Indianapolis* had a special mission and that the ship was to be prepared to sail on July 16.

As was often the case with an extended shipyard period, there was considerable turnover among the crew, with an estimated 25 percent of her enlisted complement being replaced.

At about noon on July 15, *Indianapolis* tied up at Hunters Point and a large crate was placed aboard and secured in the port hangar, where a Marine guard was posted around the clock. A smaller container, about 3 feet tall and 2 feet square, was welded to the deck of the admiral's cabin. Later it was learned that this canister contained the bomb core.

After the successful Trinity test, the first nuclear explosion in the desert, on the morning of July 16, *Indianapolis* was given orders to get underway, which she did at 0800.

According to Medical Officer Lewis Haynes, the day after *Indianapolis* sailed, he signed a dispatch as a member of Adm. Spruance's staff that stated *Indianapolis* was "under the command of the Commander in Chief" and "was not to be diverted from her mission for any reason whatsoever."

Bad weather the first day limited her speed to 28 knots, but during the next two days this was increased to 29 knots. She arrived off Diamond Head seventy-four and a half hours later, setting a speed record. *Indianapolis* was given immediate admission into the harbor. The ship was in harbor for six hours refueling, and no crew were allowed off the ship for any reason. From Pearl Harbor, *Indianapolis* and her secret cargo were ordered to proceed to Tinian, arriving on the morning of July 26. There, the secret cargo, which the world would soon learn consisted of components of the Little Boy atomic bomb that would soon be dropped on Hiroshima, Japan, was delivered.

Nine members of the crew of *Indianapolis* were killed in the March 31, 1945, kamikaze attack. All of them were interred on Kerama Retto in three separate committal services, on March 31 and April 1 and 2. Here, pallbearers are carrying the flag-draped remains of two crewmen across the well deck to a boarding ladder, for transfer to a boat that will carry the remains to the island. The Marine honor guard is at attention in the foreground. *US Naval Institute / Alfred J. Sedivi Collection*

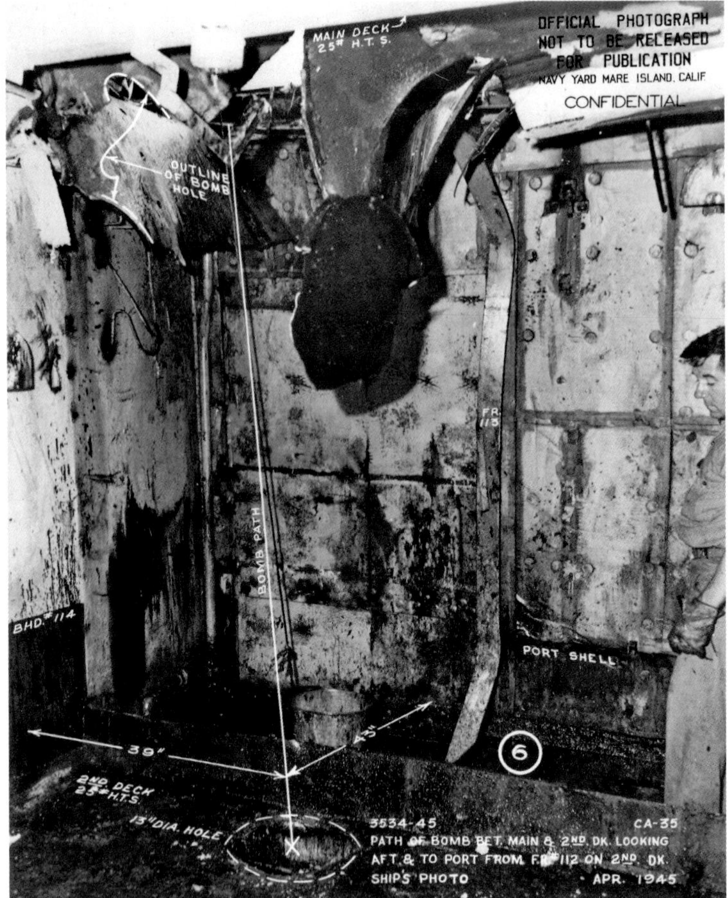

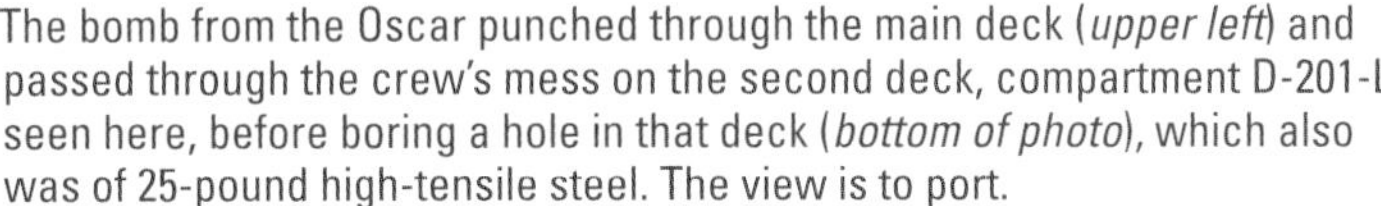

The bomb from the Oscar punched through the main deck (*upper left*) and passed through the crew's mess on the second deck, compartment D-201-L, seen here, before boring a hole in that deck (*bottom of photo*), which also was of 25-pound high-tensile steel. The view is to port.

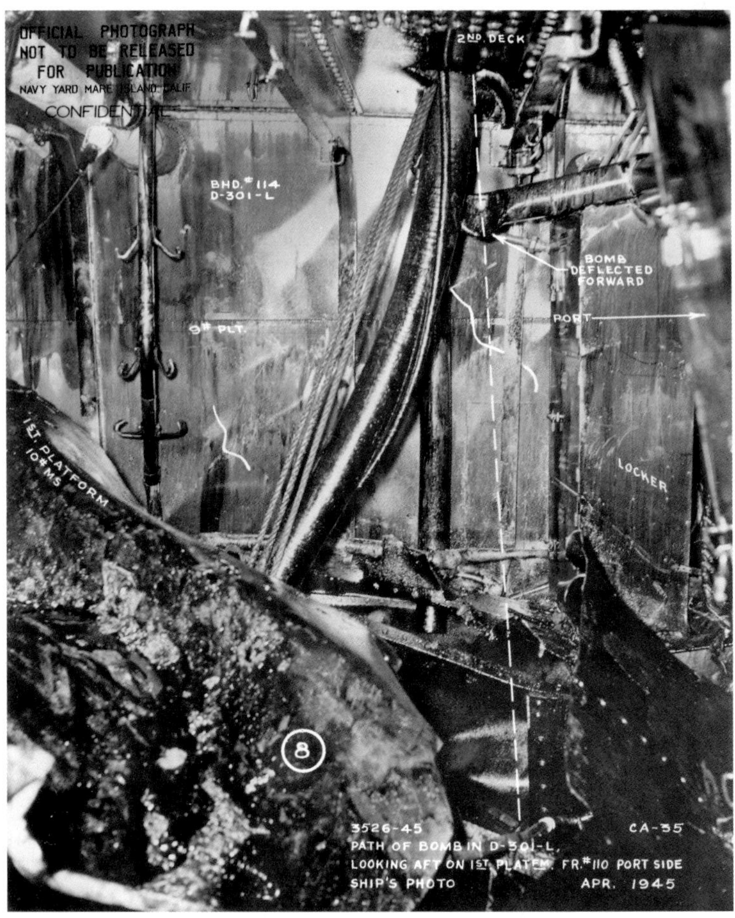

To the lower left is a piece of the first platform that was peeled back as the bomb plunged through. After punching through the second deck, the bomb passed through the crew's quarters, compartment D-301-L, making wreckage of crew lockers and berths.

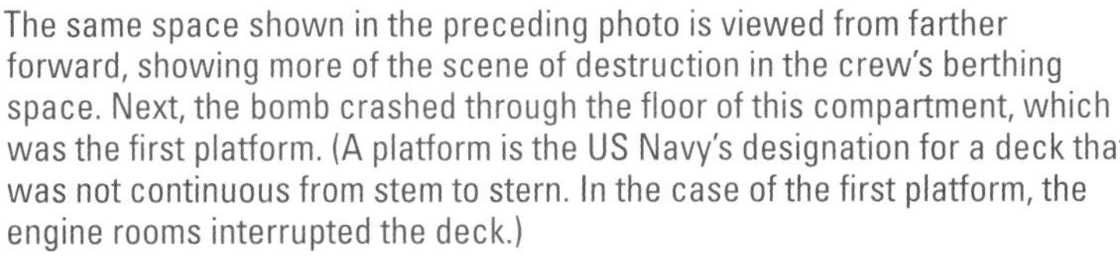

The same space shown in the preceding photo is viewed from farther forward, showing more of the scene of destruction in the crew's berthing space. Next, the bomb crashed through the floor of this compartment, which was the first platform. (A platform is the US Navy's designation for a deck that was not continuous from stem to stern. In the case of the first platform, the engine rooms interrupted the deck.)

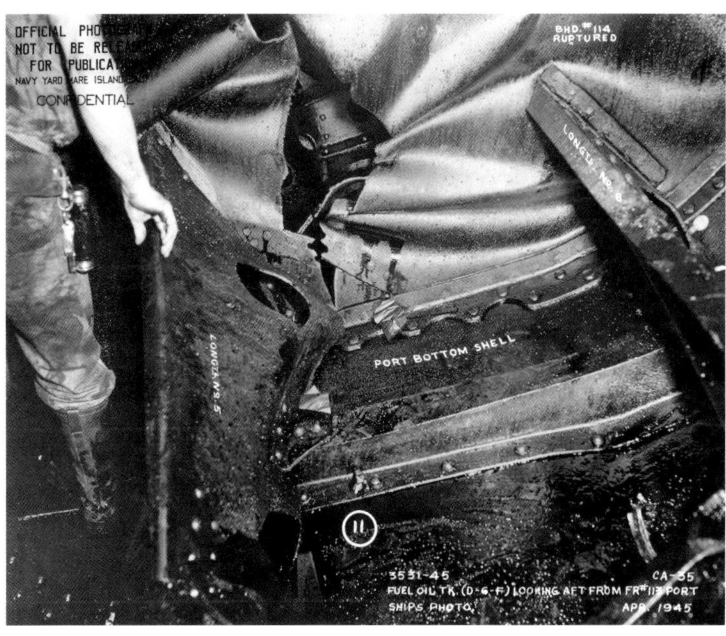

In another view inside fuel-oil tank D-6-F, facing aft from frame 113 on the port side of the ship, at the upper center is a rupture in bulkhead number 114. Indicated at the center of the photo is the port bottom shell.

After penetrating the first platform, the Japanese bomb continued on its path, crashing through this fuel-oil tank (designated compartment D-6-F). The view is facing forward and inboard from frame 113. At the time the bomb penetrated the ship, this tank was approximately 95 percent full of fuel oil.

Damage to the starboard catapult caused by the Curtiss SOC being torn loose

In a view facing aft down at the well deck below the catapults, the Curtiss SOC Seagull (side number 10) that had been on the starboard catapult at the time of the kamikaze attack on March 31, 1945, was thrown off the catapult by the force of the impact on the ship, damaging SOC number 9 (*right*) and landing upside down on the deck to the front of the starboard hangar door.

Crewmen inspect damage to SOC number 9 following the kamikaze attack. The right wing, damaged from the impact of SOC number 10 falling on it, has been folded back. The upper right wing had been smashed from the tip to the interplane struts. *US Naval Institute / Alfred J. Sedivi Collection*

The remains of one of the damaged Curtiss SOCs has been placed into one of the hangars. Lying on the deck to the right is a float. *US Naval Institute / Alfred J. Sedivi Collection*

After receiving temporary repairs at Kerama Retto, and then more at Guam, *Indianapolis* steamed under her own power to the Mare Island Navy Yard, California, for permanent repairs. In a photo of the ship in drydock at Mare Island, the port side of the hull is viewed from aft of the port inboard propeller. The dark area on the hull farther forward is from the blast of the Japanese bomb, which exploded just after exiting the hull. This area of indentation was extensive, running fore and aft from frames 104 to 122, and vertically from the keel to 15 feet below the main deck. The bomb blast damaged the port outboard propeller shaft; during temporary repairs before the ship arrived at Mare Island, much of that shaft as well as the port outboard propeller was lost. *US Naval Institute / Alfred J. Sedivi Collection*

A photo of the ship in drydock at Mare Island on May 5, 1945, shows the inward denting of the bottom of the port side of the hull from the explosion of the Japanese bomb. The bomb exited just outboard of where the forward strut of the port outboard propeller shaft was anchored (this was designated propeller number 4). The explosion tore the forward strut from the hull and severed the propeller shaft from the V-shaped aft struts, the remnants of which are shown here.

The damaged area on the port side of the hull is viewed facing aft on May 5, 1945. Indicated above the broken-off forward strut of shaft 4 are patches that had been placed over the hole where the strut broke off and, above it, the hole where the Japanese bomb punched through the bottom of the hull.

This photo taken in drydock at Mare Island on May 5, 1945, documents the damage to the bottom of the port side of the hull, farther to the rear than the preceding photo and facing forward. In the background are the severed rear struts for shaft number 4. To the right is shaft number 3, for the inboard port propeller. The official report of the kamikaze attack on *Indianapolis* likened the effect of the bomb exploding below the hull to that of a small torpedo. The extensive denting of the hull from the bomb blast is visible in the background.

The two patches over the holes in the hull are seen close-up from the side. Indicated in white print above the bomb hole are frame numbers.

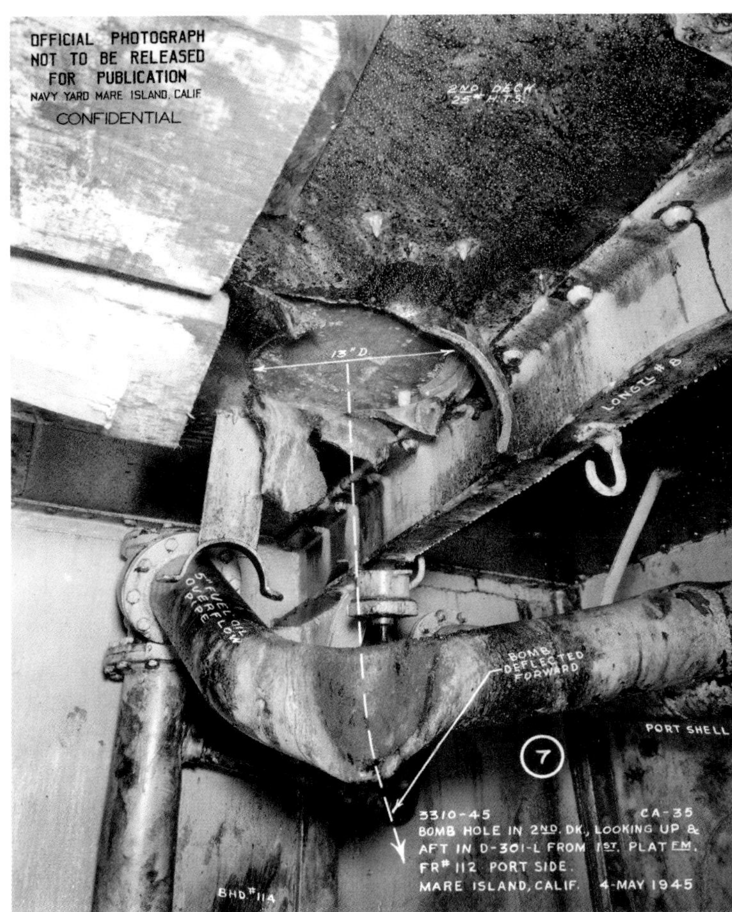

As photographed facing up and aft in the crew's quarters, compartment D-301-L on the first platform, at Mare Island on May 4, 1945, the bomb hole on the second deck has been temporarily patched, at the center of the photo. When the bomb passed through this compartment, it struck the 5-inch fuel-overflow pipe in the lower half of the photo, which deflected the trajectory of the bomb forward.

The same compartment seen in the preceding photo, D-301-L, is viewed from farther forward, facing aft, on May 4, 1945. The bent fuel-overflow pipe seen in the preceding photo is in the background, above the center of the photo. In the foreground is frame 110. The steel plates of the platform have been removed, exposing the twisted deck beams.

This view in the crew's quarters, D-301-L, was taken from the same vantage point as the preceding photo, but looking inboard. Frame 110 is again in the upper foreground. Crew lockers, some of them damaged, are to the left.

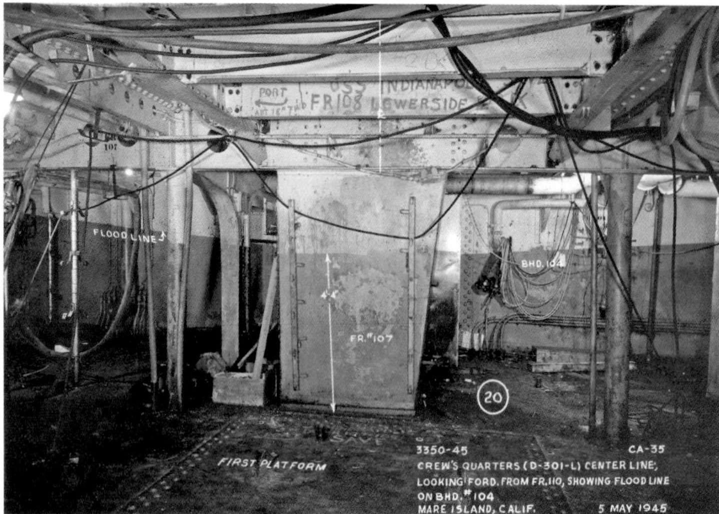

After the kamikaze attack on *Indianapolis,* parts of the interior of the ship around the bomb's trajectory flooded, but the crew was able to contain the flooding until temporary repairs could be made. In a May 4, 1945, photo of the crew's quarters facing forward at the centerline of the ship, the dark areas on the bulkheads in the background mark the extent of the flooding.

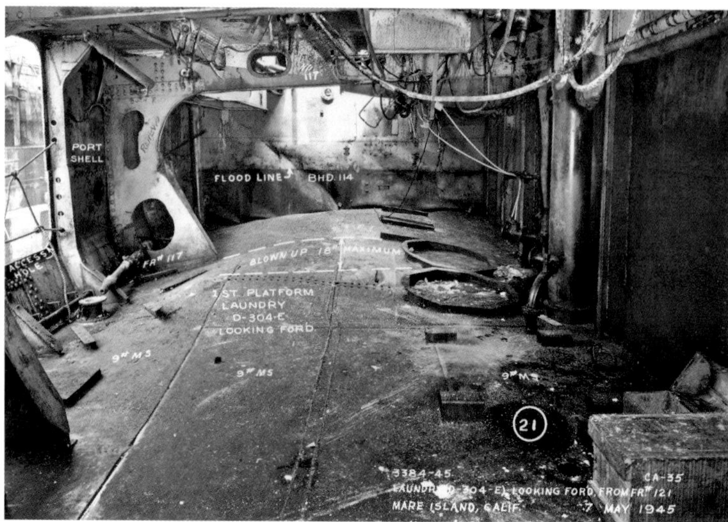

On the port side of the first platform, aft of the crew's quarters, was the laundry room. In a view in the laundry facing forward from frame 121, the bomb blast caused the floor plates to bulge upward as much as 18 inches. For repair purposes, the access hole to the far left was cut into the shell of the hull.

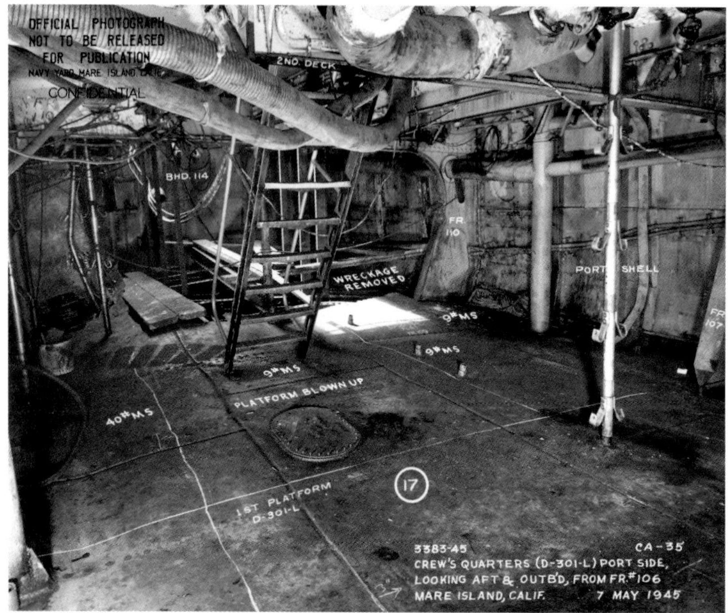

In the port side of the crew's quarters on the first platform, facing aft and outboard, the area where the Japanese bomb penetrated is in the center background. The view was taken at frame 106. In the foreground are floor plates that were buckled upward from the bomb blast.

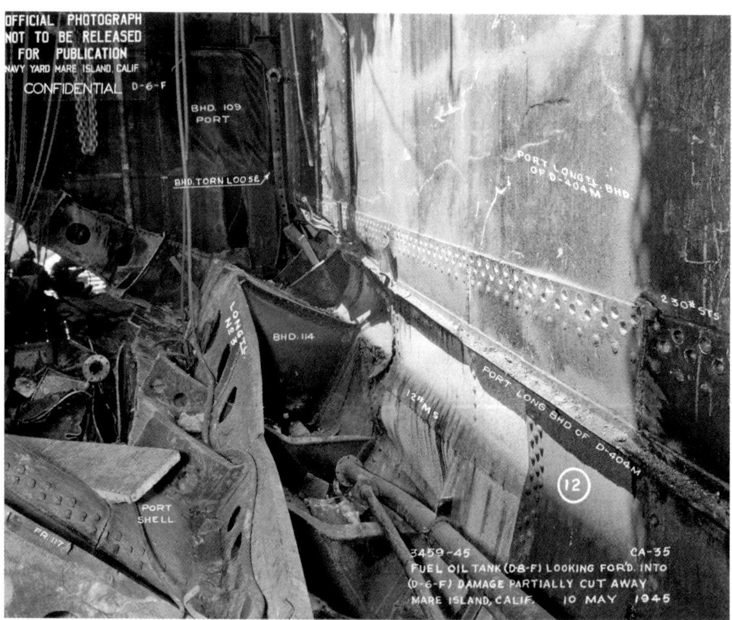

The fuel-oil tank that the Japanese bomb plummeted through is seen facing forward, with some of the damaged structures cut away. To the right is the longitudinal bulkhead on the inboard side of the tank.

On May 20, 1945, this photograph facing forward was taken to document the extent of *Indianapolis*'s structure that was removed from the port side of the hull, in preparation for permanent repairs. To the right, the locations of the second and first platforms are indicated. Toward the top, to the left of center, the second and main decks are indicated. Just forward of the ladder is part of propeller shaft number 3.

The same area of removed hull structure depicted in the preceding photo is viewed from the front facing aft on May 20, 1945. At the top is the underside of the main deck.

The part of the port hull where the bomb-damaged structures were removed at Mare Island is viewed from the side of the ship on May 20, 1945. Scaffolding has been erected on the floor of the drydock for the workers. To help support and stabilize the hull during the repair process, two pipes have been attached to brackets on the side of the hull; they are visible above the scaffold planks in the left half of the photo. *Mare Island Museum*

In a final photo taken at Mare Island on May 20, 1945, the cutaway portion of the hull is viewed from the inside, facing forward. To the left is part of the number 3 shaft, which was damaged by the bomb blast and was replaced at Mare Island. The shaft tunnel for propeller number 3 is at the lower right. *Mare Island Museum*

In addition to receiving major repairs to her hull and internal compartments at Mare Island in the spring and early summer of 1945, USS *Indianapolis* also received the latest improvements in antiaircraft weapons, radar, communications gear, and electronics. Circles on the forecastle deck are two new twin 20 mm gun mounts in two splinter shields, which replaced four single 20 mm gun mounts in two splinter shields at this location. Circled above the forward main-battery director is a fairing referred to as a shield, over the fire-control radar. Below this feature, a new electronics pod is circled. *US Navy via A. D. Baker III*

The refitted *Indianapolis* is seen from another angle. Circled aft of turret 2 is one of the new, twin 20 mm antiaircraft guns. The starboard catapult had been removed, to offset the weight of new weapons and equipment that had been installed on the ship. The object circled just below the US flag on the fantail was a fire-control radar with a dish antenna, seen in profile, installed over a quadruple 40 mm gun mount. On the platform for the SG surface-search radar atop the mainmast, a short mast topped by a direction-finder antenna was added. *US Navy via A. D. Baker III*

During the renovations at Mare Island following the kamikaze attack in 1945, the Curtiss SOC scout planes were replaced by the new Curtiss SC-1 Seahawk single-seat scout planes. Two of them, side numbers 10 and 11, are being moved into the hangars in this July 12, 1945, photograph. Circled on the mainmast near the top of the photo are two new radar direction-finder pods at each end of a catwalk. A new ladder has been installed inboard of the port hangar door. It was in the port hangar that a 15-foot-long wooden crate containing the "cannon" component of the "Little Boy" atomic bomb, which would be dropped on Hiroshima less than a month later, would soon be stored, guarded by Marines, during the voyage from Hunters Point, San Francisco, to Tinian. *US Navy via A. D. Baker III*

In a photo from the rear of the forward smokestack to the bow, to the lower left is a spare center float for an SC-1 Seahawk. The object circled in the 40 mm director tub at the starboard aft corner of the navigating bridge a Mk. 51 director covered in canvas. *US Navy via A. D. Baker III*

Indianapolis was photographed from just above the water at an angle of 45 degrees from her longitudinal centerline off Mare Island on July 10, 1945. The ship remained in the Measure 22 camouflage scheme, although in February 1945 the formulation of the paints changed slightly and became neutral colors. Thus, the Haze Gray (5-H) in this photo is neutral, and lacked the purple/blue cast of the earlier 5-H. Also, the decks were Deck Gray (20), not deck blue. The absence of the starboard catapult is noticeable. *US Navy via A. D. Baker III*

The cruiser is viewed from broadside on the starboard beam while at anchor on July 10, 1945. Twenty days later, the ship would be sunk.

Indianapolis is observed from astern off Mare Island, California, on July 10, 1945. Jutting from the sides of the hull are the propeller guards.

Indianapolis is viewed from the starboard side, 135 degrees off the longitudinal centerline of the ship, just above the water. As successive modernizations added more height and weight to the superstructure and the masts, Fifth Fleet commander Adm. Raymond Spruance, who made *Indianapolis* his flagship, reportedly opined that if the ship were ever struck by a torpedo, the high center of gravity would result in her capsizing and sinking.

In a view of the ship from off the port beam on July 10, 1945, the forward Mk. 33 director, above the navigating bridge, is trained to starboard, while the aft Mk. 33 is trained to port. At this distance, the Mk. 25 dish antenna is not discernible on the front of that director.

A final photo of *Indianapolis* anchored off Mare Island on July 10, 1945, was taken off the bow. Soon thereafter, the cruiser departed Mare Island and proceeded to Hunters Point Naval Shipyard, where atomic-bomb components were taken aboard for delivery to Tinian. In addition to the crate with the "cannon" for the atomic bomb stored in the port hangar, a lead canister containing the uranium projectile for the bomb was welded to the floor of the flag staff's quarters. *Indianapolis* departed from Hunters Point for Tinian on July 16, the same date the first atomic weapon was successfully detonated, at Trinity Site, New Mexico. *US Navy via A. D. Baker III*

Indianapolis is in the harbor at Tinian on or around July 26, 1945, on which date she delivered the top-secret atomic-bomb components, along with about one hundred civilians connected to the Manhattan Project, the US program to develop the atomic bomb. A Curtiss SC is on the catapult, and another one, wings folded, is on the deck below. *Naval History and Heritage Command*

CHAPTER 4

Indianapolis: Lost . . . and Found

With her cargo offloaded, *Indianapolis* was ordered to Guam, steaming through the night and arriving about 1000. Reprovisioned, she sailed from Guam on Saturday morning, July 28, at about 0930, bound for Leyte. Because there had been none of the customary post-shipyard training, and little chance for training during the transit to Tinian, McVay wanted to approach Leyte during morning hours so as to have the best chance for antiaircraft practice. To do so, *Indianapolis* would either have to steam at 24–25 knots and arrive on the morning of the thirtieth, or at an average of 15.7 knots and arrive on the morning of the thirty-first. Having just punished both the ship and crew with ten days of hard steaming from the mainland, McVay opted for the slower pace, planning to arrive at Leyte at 1100 on Tuesday, July 31. The route dictated by the Port Director Guam was a commonly used one, known as Route Peddie.

In a series of circumstances that remain controversial to this day, reports of Japanese submarine activity did not reach *Indianapolis* or any of those parties directly influencing its course, speed, or operation.

This is significant, because US Navy zigzag tactical doctrine of the time prescribed that ships should zigzag "during good visibility, including bright moonlight, in areas where enemy submarines may be encountered." On the fateful night of July 29, there was intermittent moonlight, and the Navy had indicated that there was no serious threat of enemy submarine activity. Accordingly, *Indianapolis* discontinued zigzagging after dark.

Unknown to the crew on the *Indianapolis*, on July 28 Japanese submarine *I-58* had attacked two US navy ships. About thirty hours later, at 2305 on July 29, 1945, Commander Mochitsura Hashimoto surfaced *I-58* and, scanning the horizon, was surprised to see *Indianapolis*, which he believed to be an Idaho-class battleship, looming 10,000 meters away. Quickly diving, Hashimoto ordered *I-58* to prepare to launch a torpedo attack. At 2356 he began firing six torpedoes at *Indianapolis* at a range of 1500 meters and a target angle of 60 degrees starboard. The last of six torpedoes left *I-58* at 0002. At 0003 on July 30, Hashimoto noted a torpedo hit abreast the number 1 turret starboard, followed in his estimation by at least two more hits, and at 0004 his target came to a stop. On July 30 he radioed a report of his successful sinking of a battleship to his command in Kure.

US intelligence intercepted Hashimoto's report of the sinking but discounted it, believing that *I-58* herself had been sunk on July 22.

In the center background, USS *Indianapolis* is in the harbor at Tinian around July 26, 1945. The view is facing south from the southern end of the island, with Aguijan Island in the distance. At Tinian, the atomic-bomb components were delivered to personnel of the 1st Ordnance Squadron, Special (Aviation), part of the 509th Composite Group, tasked with delivering the bomb to targets in Japan. The photographs taken at Tinian are the last known photos of *Indianapolis. Naval History and Heritage Command*

Aboard *Indianapolis*, the first torpedo had torn the bow off at frame 7. After the second Type 95 torpedo tore into *Indianapolis* at about frame 46, she had lost virtually all electrical power, her communications systems were knocked out (as were engines 1, 2, and 4), and smoke and flames began to fill the air.

Capt. McVay, thrown from his bunk by the blast, made his way the few steps to the bridge and had learned that the ship was dark, and with internal communications out the bridge did not know the nature of the attack or the extent of the damage. *Indianapolis* had taken on a 3-degree list and was still underway. On the basis of his experience with *Indianapolis* off Okinawa, McVay did not deem it necessary to abandon ship. Within three minutes, however, that would change, when executive officer Cmdr. Flynn reported to the captain, "We are definitely going down, and I suggest that we abandon ship." Confident in his XO's abilities and judgment, McVay immediately ordered, "Pass the word to abandon ship," and with internal communications out, passing the word was literally how this had to be handled.

When he first appeared on the bridge, McVay had ordered a distress signal be sent out. After ordering "Abandon ship," McVay personally went to the radio room to confirm that this had happened. The radio operator would later testify that he had signaled the ship's distress, but he was uncertain if the message had gotten out due to the loss of power.

Just as McVay reached the communications deck, the starboard list, which been increasing steadily, reached 90 degrees. Twelve minutes after the first torpedo hit, *Indianapolis* was on her side. Within moments, she would first roll over, then stand vertical, and then bow down, before rapidly descending into the Pacific.

It is estimated that two hundred to three hundred of her crew went with her, either dead before she sank, trapped belowdecks or on deck in the wreckage, or pulled down by the suction of the sinking ship.

There remained that evening about eight hundred survivors, many covered in bunker oil that had escaped from their sinking ship, some severely injured, and a few in life rafts. Many had on kapok life vests or clung to life nets; some treaded water.

It is estimated that of the initial group of survivors, about a hundred succumbed to their injuries within the first few hours.

For four days the men drifted in the sea, with dehydration, exposure, and exhaustion taking a steady toll on the survivors. In desperation, some drank salt water, with fatal consequences. Delirium and hallucinations caused some men to attack others. Sharks, probably initially attracted by the sound of the blasts and the dead in the water, soon began approaching the survivors, attacking some.

Remarkably, no one noticed that the ship was overdue at Leyte. Thus it was not until 1025 on August 2 that the survivors were found, and that was by chance, rather than by search. Lt. Wilbur Gwinn in a PV-1 patrol bomber was wrestling with a malfunctioning trailing antenna when he spotted an oil slick. Hoping he was on to a crippled enemy submarine, he descended, only to learn that it was a vast oil slick, clearly from a large vessel, and that there were many survivors, apparently American, in the water. Gwinn dropped a sonar buoy and a life raft and radioed his findings. A PBY-5A flown by Lt. Adrian Marks and a second PV-1 flown by Lt. Cmdr. George Atteberry, commander of Patrol Bombing Squadron 152, immediately launched from Palau, the faster PV-1 passing the PBY en route.

After surveying the scene at the direction of Atteberry, Marks began dropping survival gear, directed toward groups of men who had nothing but life jackets. At 1630, Marks made the decision to set his amphibian PBY-5A Catalina down in order to recover individuals who were not in groups. This decision was made despite standing orders not to attempt an open sea landing. The landing was rough because of heavy swells, but ultimately Marks picked up fifty-six badly wounded survivors, who were both placed inside the aircraft and lashed atop the wings. Marks's aircraft was joined by a second PBY, an Army OA-10 flown by 1Lt. Richard C. Alcorn, but he unfortunately was able to pick up only one survivor.

At 2315 the 24-inch searchlight of the destroyer escort *Cecil J. Doyle* (DE-368), commanded by W. Graham Claytor Jr., was sighted. This was risky, considering the obvious submarine presence, but Claytor had turned on the searchlight to inspire survivors and aid pilots in locating their position. *Cecil J. Doyle* was brought near the PBY, and the ship's boat was used to retrieve the survivors and crew from the now badly damaged PBY as well as to rescue men in the water. Following World War II, Claytor became president of Southern Railway, serving from 1967 to 1977, when he resigned to become secretary of the Navy, and he was later appointed deputy secretary of defense. Claytor radioed higher command that the survivors were from the cruiser *Indianapolis*.

Cecil J. Doyle was joined by *Bassett* (APD-73), *Dufilho* (DE-423), *Ringness* (APD-100), *Register* (APD-92), *Madison* (DD-425), and *Ralph Talbot* (DD-390).

Ultimately, 316 men of the 1,195 crew were plucked from the water, although two of these succumbed shortly thereafter. Early, and oft-repeated, reports stating there were 317 survivors were predicated on the belief that Radio Technician 2nd Class Clarence Donnor was aboard, when in fact he had been transferred off the ship at Mare Island, a mere one hour after having been transferred onto the ship. Also recovered were ninety-one bodies, only about half of which could be identified. Among the survivors was Captain McVay, who was picked up at 1300 on August 3 by *Ringness*.

An inquiry was held on Guam on August 13, which found that Capt. McVay "incurred serious blame" for the loss, and recommended he be tried by general court martial. The charges were "culpable inefficiency in the performance of his duty" and "negligently endangering the lives of others."

The commander in chief of the US Pacific Fleet, Adm. Chester Nimitz, disagreed with these findings and refused to approve them. However, the chief of naval operations, Earnest King, supported moving ahead with a general court-martial. The specific charges laid out were "through negligence suffering a vessel of the navy to be hazarded" and "culpable inefficiency in the performance of duty." While the second charge was ruled "not proved," the court found McVay guilty of the first, despite testimony both of Japanese commander Hashimoto and veteran US submarine captain Glynn Donaho (who himself had sunk twenty-three enemy vessels, all zigzagging) that had *Indianapolis* been zigzagging, the outcome would have been no different.

Capt. McVay was sentenced to lose 100 numbers in his temporary grade of captain and 100 numbers in his permanent grade of commander. The vast majority of the survivors considered the court-martial of their captain an outrage, and the verdict even more so. A few families of the lost felt the verdict was justified.

McVay was restored to duty, although never again a sea command, until he retired in 1949. The loss of so many of his men, and the attack on his character, weighed heavily on him, and he died by suicide on November 6, 1968, a gun in one hand and a toy sailor in the other.

On August 18, 2017, late billionaire Paul G. Allen's research ship *Petrel* found *Indianapolis* 3,000 fathoms down, resting in two large pieces on the floor of the North Pacific.

Father Thomas Conway was a Catholic curate in Buffalo, New York, when he enlisted in the US Navy in September 1942. He became a chaplain on USS *Indianapolis* in 1944 and is seen here conducting mass next to a turret on that cruiser. Father Conway was on the ship when it was torpedoed, and was among those who were able to abandon the ship. For three days and nights he swam from group to group of crewmen, offering solace and support and administering last rites to sailors as they passed away. On the third night, he became delirious, eventually slipping below the surface to his death. *US Naval Institute / Alfred J. Sedivi Collection*

After making its secret delivery to Tinian and a brief stop at Guam, *Indianapolis* proceeded without escort toward Leyte, Philippine Islands. During the voyage she was torpedoed and sunk by the Japanese submarine *I-58*. Here, some of the survivors of the sinking of USS *Indianapolis* are being brought ashore from the hospital ship USS *Tranquility* (AH-14) at Guam on August 18, 1945. Dodge WC-54 ambulances will take them from the dock to local hospitals for treatment.

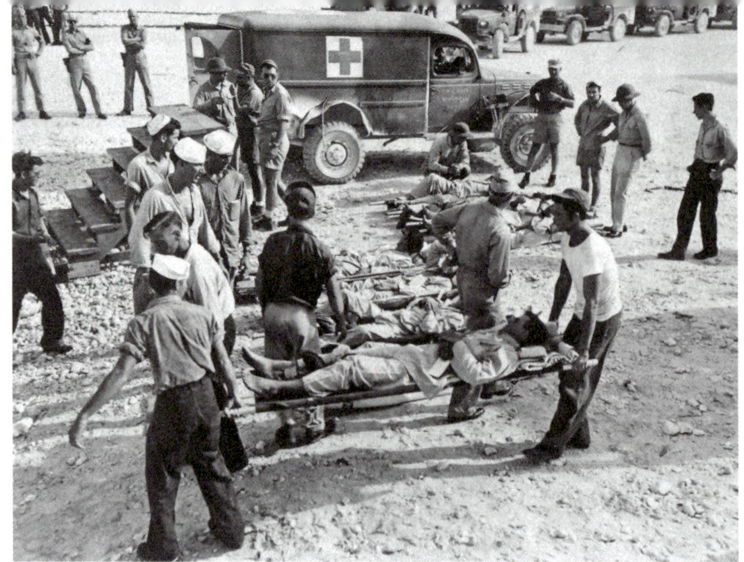

Ambulances are lined up to transport survivors of *Indianapolis* to a hospital. This appears to have been on Peleliu, since the cab door on the closest Dodge WC-54 is marked for USN Base Hospital No. 20, which was located on that island.

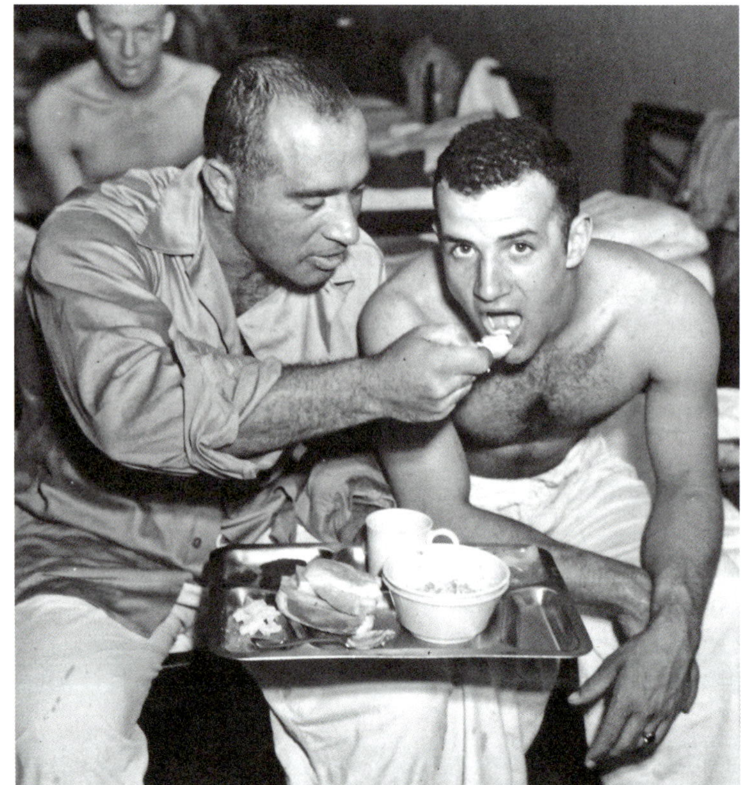

A survivor of the *Indianapolis* sinking helps feed a fellow survivor in a hospital on Peleliu, while a gaunt-looking survivor looks on in the background.

Gunner's Mate 3rd Class Robert Lee Shipman, US Navy Reserve, survived the sinking of *Indianapolis* but died on Peleliu after his rescue. With the flag at half staff in the background, a funeral party is escorting GM3C Shipman's remains to a cemetery on Peleliu on August 15, 1945. Subsequently, his remains were repatriated and buried in Stilwell Cemetery, Stilwell, Oklahoma.

Japanese submarine *I-58*, which sunk *Indianapolis*, survived the war and is seen here at Kure Harbor, Japan, on October 16, 1945, two and a half months after her fatal encounter with *Indianapolis*. Nested next to her on the starboard side and partially visible is *I-53*.

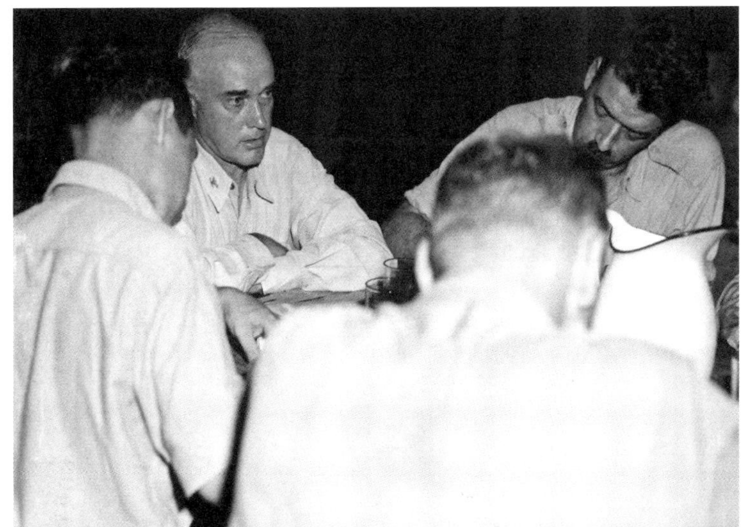

Capt. Charles B. McVay III, the commanding officer of *Indianapolis* at the time of her sinking, was a survivor. Here, he is holding a press conference with correspondents on Guam in August 1945. Capt. McVay was court-martialed and convicted for failure to have *Indianapolis* follow a zigzag course at the time of the torpedoing. He retired from the Navy in 1949 and committed suicide in 1968. The US Congress passed a resolution in October 2000 exonerating Capt. McVay; President Clinton endorsed the resolution, and the document is part of his Navy file.

I-58 was photographed from the starboard side while docked at Sasebo Naval Arsenal on January 28, 1946. In early April of that year, all usable equipment was removed from *I-58*, and she was towed out to sea and blown up. In 2017, a 200-foot-long section of *I-58* was discovered and its identity confirmed, 600 feet below the surface of the East China Sea.

The remnants of USS *Indianapolis* were discovered at a depth of about 18,000 feet in the Philippine Sea on August 19, 2017, by a team sponsored by Paul Allen, cofounder of Microsoft, on the research vessel *Petrel.* A camera on a remotely controlled underwater vehicle recorded the wreckage. Despite spending seventy-two years in salt water, the white paint and stenciled markings are remarkably well preserved on this spare-parts box discovered near the wreckage. *Courtesy of Paul G. Allen*

Part of the scoreboard from the bridge of *Indianapolis* was discovered, including nine Japanese flags signifying aircraft the ship shot down. This was part of one of the side bulwarks of the navigating bridge (it's not clear if it was on the port side or the starboard side), and upon extreme magnification of the photos taken at Mare Island on July 12, 1945, it is evident that these markings are identical to the ones that existed at that date. The black airplane symbol was at the top of the scoreboard. *Courtesy of Paul G. Allen*

One of the turrets is viewed from the front left. Clearly visible on the 8-inch/55-caliber guns is the dark-colored Deck Gray (20) on the tops of the barrels, over Haze Gray (5-H) on the sides and the lower parts, per the ship's final camouflage scheme, Measure 22. *Courtesy of Paul G. Allen*

The bow section of *Indianapolis* is lying on its starboard side. The port anchor remains free of rust, with its foundry marks clearly visible. On the left side are marked "NORFOLK / HL / NAVY YARD / NORFOLK," and on the right side, "NO. 12669 / WT. 13395 / 1929 / U.S. NAVY." *Courtesy of Paul G. Allen*

On the bow section that is half-buried in sediment, the forecastle deck is shown, including the port wildcat (the capstan that operated the anchor chain), the anchor chain where it emerges from the anchor-chain locker, and the handwheels that controlled the wildcats. *Courtesy of Paul G. Allen*

The upper part of the hole from the torpedo blast at frame 46 on the starboard side of the hull, at the second deck, is depicted. *Courtesy of Paul G. Allen*

Marine growths have clung to this 5-inch/25-caliber gun mount. The muzzle, the gun carriage, and a guardrail are in view. *Courtesy of Paul G. Allen*

The blast of the torpedo that struck the hull on the starboard side at frame 46 created this exit hole on the communication platform, near the rear of turret number 2. *Courtesy of Paul G. Allen*

Indianapolis's hull number, "35," still remains visible on the port side of the bow. The dark area toward the upper left is a porthole toward the forward end of the windlass room, on the main deck. *Courtesy of Paul G. Allen*